If We Had a Boat

niversity of Utah Press · 1986 · Salt Lake City

If We Had a Boat

GREEN RIVER EXPLORERS
ADVENTURERS
AND
RUNNERS

by
Roy Webb

Bonneville Books

University of Utah Press   1986   Salt Lake City

Library of Congress Cataloging-in-Publication Data

Webb, Roy D.
  If we had a boat.

  (Bonneville books)
  Bibliography: p.
  Includes index.

  1. Green River (Wyo.-Utah)—Description and travel.
2. Green River Valley (Wyo.-Colo.)—Description and
travel. 3. Green River (Wyo.-Colo.)—History. 4. Green
River Valley (Wyo.-Utah)—History. I. Title.
F767.G7W43 1986   979.2'21   86-15846
ISBN 0-87480-261-X

Photograph Credits:

Photographs on pages 12, 16, 30, 59, 65, 128 courtesy of Dinosaur National
Monument, Department of the Interior, National Park Service; on pages 38
(Angus M. Woodbury papers), 70 (by E. O. Beaman), 85 (Utah Power and
Light Co. papers), 116 (Ray DeSpain papers), 120 (Utah Power and Light
Co. papers), 131 (Upper Colorado Grass Roots, Inc.) courtesy of Special Col-
lections, Marriott Library, University of Utah; on pages 94 (Kolb photo col-
lection) and 138 courtesy of Bureau of Reclamation, Upper Colorado Region;
on page 24 courtesy of Leo C. Thorne; on page 40 taken from William L.
Manly, *Death Valley in '49*; on page 72 (by E. O. Beaman) courtesy of Sweetwater County Historical Museum, Green River, Wyoming; on page 148 courtesy of Don Hatch; on page 151 courtesy of P. T. Reilly; on cover © John
Telford 1986.

TO

BECCI

*whose unfailing love and encouragement
made this book possible*

Contents

ILLUSTRATIONS

MAPS

Acknowledgments

Many small streams must come together to form a big river like the Green. So it has been with this book. It started as a series of informal talks given to visitors staying at the riverside campgrounds in Dinosaur National Monument. Later, as I worked on a degree in history at the University of Utah, the idea evolved into a paper for a seminar. Still later, with encouragement from various friends, I embarked on the attempt to make it into a book. The process has had its good moments and its bad, but like running rapids you learn quickly from your mistakes and are all the more ready to try it again.

This book simply would not have been written without the help and encouragement of my good friend Mike Brown. Mike and I have shared many a warm beer at various riverside camps, and it was during such discussions that the initial ideas for this work took shape. Mike shares a love of river history and has served as a sounding board for many of my ideas, and has contributed not a few himself. I am grateful to him for that and many other things.

My co-workers and supervisors in Special Collections, Marriott Library, University of Utah, deserve a great note of thanks. Having a research library specializing in Western Americana at my fingertips, as it were, has made this project infinitely simpler. Besides the ease of access, many persons in Special Collections have helped. Dr. Gregory C. Thompson, the Director of Special Collections, has been a source of encouragement and a great deal more during the course of this book.

His knowledge of publishing, of the ways of university presses and committees, and of western American history, have aided me immeasurably. He has also given me a receptive shoulder during those times of discouragement that any author (especially a new author) faces. Nancy V. Young, the Manuscripts Librarian and my supervisor, has also been a great source of support, with her humor and patience and goodwill, as has Walter Jones, Reference Librarian in Western Americana. My co-workers in the Manuscripts Division, Marcie, Allesen, and Karin, have if nothing else listened to endless river stories with great patience. The same goes for many other people in the Marriott Library. Thank you all.

The staff of the University of Utah Press has supported this project almost from the start by offering innumerable suggestions and much encouragement. Dr. Brigham Madsen, one of my heroes among western American historians (''When I grow up I want to write history like him''), read the manuscript in the early stages and offered many excellent suggestions. Another source of encouragement and good editorial suggestions has been Cort Conley of the University of Idaho Press. Cort, besides being a good editor, is also very knowledgeable in river history and caught many of the errors inherent in a work like this. He has read the manuscript in several forms and has been supportive from the start. And Cort finally taught me how to spell rendezvous. I'd also like to thank Susan Neel for reading my section on the Echo Park Dam controversy and giving me the benefit of her years of research on that emotionally charged subject.

Students of the Colorado River tend to become very partisan about one of the two branches of the river, the Green or the Grand, although I fail to see how anyone could deny that the Green is the main stem. Dr. Gary Topping of the Utah State Historical Society helped greatly with his knowledge of many aspects of Colorado River history.

Lynn Loetterle and Linda West of Dinosaur National Monument were very helpful in providing photographs of the Dinosaur area which appear in this book. I would also like to thank Raymond DeSeyne Larlenque for providing a copy of his father's journal documenting the French kayak trip of 1938.

Finally, I want to thank my wife Becci. When we got engaged, about the same time I started on this book, the closest she had been to a river trip was a stroll along the shore of the Wansee after kaffe und kuchen in her native Berlin. Now she has run big rapids with me, endured sand, mosquitoes, and other unpleasant aspects of river camping, and has, more than anyone else, supported me through the good and the bad moments.

If We Had a Boat

Introduction

Rivers have played a major part in the life and history of many places, and yet rivers have a life and a history all their own. They are at once avenue and obstruction; source of life and bringer of destruction, cursed by pioneers and idolized by poets. Pioneer or poet, few can stand by the bank of a river, look upstream and not wonder about its origins, what the river passes in its course.

When Franciscans Dominguez and Escalante and their grumbling crew crossed the San Buenaventura in September 1776 after asking the protection of the "Thrice-Holy Saints," they could have had no idea that the "copious" river would loom so large in the pages of the history of the American West. They could not have known, for instance, that a generation of western travelers and explorers would search across the western United States for the mythical river that Don Miera y Pacheco was so certain led to the Pacific Coast. Nor could they have known that even as they crossed the river, forces were in motion that would through a roundabout way bring General William Ashley and his crew of trappers down that same river scarcely fifty years later.

Even though John C. Frémont had proved that the San Buenaventura—the long sought after passage to the Pacific—was no more than wishful thinking, the myth still had a strong hold on men's minds. America had every other sort of natural advantage—rich farmlands, temperate climates, enough land for all—why not a route to California just as the Ohio had been into Kentucky and the Missouri into the Plains?

The first people to run the Green River were the trappers who accompanied General William Ashley in search of fur and a place of "rendavose." Ashley had been in the fur trade for three disastrous years when he came to the banks of the Green River in 1825. Ashley came to the country around the Green River, long known as prime trapping grounds, to try and recoup the losses he had suffered along the Missouri. Reasoning that where there was water there must be beaver, Ashley floated the river in boats made of buffalo skins.

Less than a quarter century later, William Manly and his fellow forty-niners saw the river as a shortcut to the California gold fields. As they found out to their sorrow, it was anything but a shortcut. Twenty years after Manly, John Wesley Powell, a one-armed, determined former artillery officer in the Civil War, wanted to conduct the first scientific survey of the river and its canyons, to map the river and plot its fall. He was one of the first to approach the river on its own terms. Powell saw the Green and the Colorado as scientific problems to be solved through investigation, with barometer, sextant, and compass, and attempted to define the river in physical terms. Powell's two voyages were largely successful in this; after him the river was mapped and plotted, its course traced, the canyons measured, and the fall of the river determined. Unavoidably, however, he too fell under the spell of the river, and contrary to his purpose ended up adding yet more to the aura of danger and hardship that had surrounded the Green since men first began traveling down it.

It was not until a simple trapper and prospector who lived near the banks of the Green decided that there must be a way to go down the river in reasonable safety that the old myths began to die. Nathaniel Galloway was certainly not out to shatter any myths, though. Like Manly before him, he was after gold; like Ashley, he sought furs. But it was Galloway's pursuit of such riches that finally opened the river to regular travel. The flat-bottomed Galloway boat, and more importantly his stern-first method of running rapids, revolutionized river travel. Before him, a journey down the Green was regarded as a "real escapade—difficult, tedious and hard," something that a man had better approach with his wits about him and his will written. Galloway proved that almost anyone could run the river and live to tell about it; he did it, in fact, until he was almost seventy years old.

The secret of running rivers might have died with him in 1913, however, if it had not been for the efforts of Julius Stone and the Kolb brothers, Ellsworth and Emery. While Galloway did write up some of his experiences, these did not see wide circulation. The Kolb brothers' *Through the Grand Canyon from Wyoming to Mexico,* as well as Stone's later *Canyon Country,* did. More than anyone else, they brought home to readers the beauties of the Green and the Colorado and the fact that yes, men did go down the river and yes, they did it without incredible hardship and danger. When it became known that the Kolbs were complete amateurs, who had never run any river anywhere before, the legend of the "unrunnable" Green began to fade.

But while some men began to see beauty and adventure in the canyons, others looked and saw something entirely different. Soon after the beginning of the twentieth century, the newly created Reclamation Service and the infant electrical utilities began to send survey parties down the Green and its tributaries to identify sites for hydroelectric dams. Even though their voyages were not heralded in the papers, as were those undertaken solely for adventure, in the end they would turn out to be by far the more significant. The engineers' choice of the confluence of the Green and the Yampa as the site for a dam would precipitate one of the most bitter and protracted conservation disputes of the century. The compromise agreed to by both sides of that struggle would in turn lead to the damming of the Green in Red Canyon, changing forever the character of Flaming Gorge, Horseshoe, and Kingfisher canyons, and indeed the entire river.

The twentieth century also saw the first river runners who floated the Green for no other reason than just to do it. It seemed that everyone before had to have a reason to run the river, whether it was furs or gold or knowledge. In the 1920s, some began to float the Green for the adventure and the challenge of running rapids. Finally, around this same time, others realized that here was something that some might pay to do. In the early 1930s, a number of different men began to take passengers down the river for pay, and the Green saw its first tourists. It was not until after the Second World War, however, that tourism became big business on the Green. Indirectly, that terrible conflict provided the technological tools and impetus needed to bring river running into the modern age, both in terms of the type of boats used and eventually the numbers of people on the river. Just as Galloway's boats had made running the Green possible, now the rubber inflatable rafts which Bus Hatch and a number of others began to use to carry scores of passengers at a time, made it profitable.

Like so many aspects of American life, the Green River is now regulated physically and legally. Parts of the canyons have been drowned by reservoirs, making the river that Ashley, Manly and Powell explored quite different, indeed. Yet there is still a challenge; still an adventure. And although the people and the boats have changed, the reasons that people run rivers have not. There will always be those who, like the adventurers before them, look at a river and think to themselves, "If we had a boat. . . ."

1

River, Rapids, and Canyons

In the mysterious shorthand of geographers and mapmakers, the Green River begins at 43°09′ north longitude 109°40′ west latitude, on the west slope of the Wind River Mountains,[1] part of the northern Rocky Mountain Cordillera that bisects the North American continent. By another method, equally arcane, the river begins in Section 28, Township 37 North, Range 107 West, in Sublette County of the state of Wyoming, United States of America. Either description, no matter how physically accurate, is much too dry to adequately convey the awe-inspiring setting in which the river makes its humble beginnings. Little Dale Lake, half-frozen most of the year, is the official source of the river, according to the U.S. Geological Survey Gannet Peak quadrangle. Other streams that tumble down the granite slopes of Mount Arrowhead, American Legion Peak, and Split Mountain contribute to its flow, but Dale Lake is the main source, where the river gathers itself before its final plunge down the mountains, out of its birthplace and to its destiny. The infant river is barely a yard wide, not even enough to hinder the traveler. The mountains around the lake are towering fangs of granite that loom over boulder-choked gorges thousands of feet deep. The narrow stream sometimes disappears beneath the boulders and permanent snowfields. Frequent lightning storms crash and thunder among the peaks. The Wind Rivers are a forbiddingly beautiful range of moun-

tains, still the haunt of grizzly, moose, and elk, and a fitting beginning
for the Green and many other major streams, including the Bighorn
River, one of the sources of the Yellowstone, and the Sweetwater, a
source of the North Platte.

After flowing through the beautiful Green River Lakes, the Green
runs north for awhile, then finally makes up its mind and turns to the
south into the plains of Wyoming. By now it has increased its volume
with the additions of the New Fork and Horse Creek and is a full-fledged
river by the standards of the arid West. It is ready for the passage through
the many canyons it has carved on its way south, a terrain different
from but no less forbidding or beautiful than its mountain origins.

The Green is 730 miles long. Almost immediately after entering
Utah, it turns east along the north slope of the Uinta Mountains into
Colorado. In the northwest corner of that state, it turns south once again,
cutting through the Uintas and then turning back to the west into Utah.
It stays in Utah and on a generally southern course for the rest of its
length. It meets its sister stream, the Colorado, in the heart of Canyon-
lands National Park.

The drainage basin of the Green is just under 45,000 square miles;
the mean annual runoff is around 5,700,000 acre-feet.[2] In terms of phys-
iographic provinces, the river begins in the northern Rocky Mountains
and ends in the Colorado Plateau, making the transition on the south
side of the Uinta Mountains. The Green traverses many life and vegetation zones in its course, ranging from alpine, above timberline, to
bare desert at its confluence with the Colorado. The wildlife found in
and along the river includes elk, moose, marmots, and trout near the
headwaters; antelope, rabbits, eagles, and hawks in the plains; and liz-
ards, rattlesnakes, catfish, and the endangered cougar, desert bighorn
sheep, and Colorado River squawfish in the lower canyons. In addition, thousands of ducks, geese, cranes, herons, and other waterfowl
use the Green as a flyway during their annual migrations. Riparian vegetation consists mostly of cottonwoods, willows, and, in the lower
stretches, tamarisk.

The Green receives the flow of many tributaries, large and small,
but here only those three lying within the area to be covered will be
discussed: Henry's Fork, the Yampa, and the White. Henry's Fork begins on the north slope of the Uinta Mountains, loops out into the plains,
and enters the Green about seventy miles below the town of Green River,
Wyoming. The lower end was flooded by Flaming Gorge Reservoir

in 1963. The mouth of Henry's Fork was a favorite wintering area for Indians, the first site chosen by William Ashley for a rendezvous of the mountain men (he later moved the rendezvous twenty miles up Henry's Fork), and the location of the little town of Linwood. The Yampa and the White begin in the western foothills of the Park Range in northwestern Colorado. Both flow west paralleling each other, the Yampa on the north, the White on the south. The Yampa empties into the Green in Echo Park, so its course is entirely within the state of Colorado. The White enters Utah and then flows into the Green about sixty miles downriver from the little town of Jensen. Each river has carved a deep canyon along its lower course, and although the Yampa's is by far the most spectacular, neither has received much attention and both still retain their wilderness character. Now, however, they are being considered by reclamation engineers for potential dam sites: the Yampa for irrigation and flood control, the White as a source of water for development of the vast beds of oil shale that it runs through. The wilderness quality they both now enjoy could change rapidly.

One stream that some think of as a tributary of the Green is the Grand, now known as the Colorado. Actually, the Green is often listed as a tributary of the Colorado. A quick check of the facts reveals the truth, however. The drainage basin of the Grand is only 26,000 square miles, just over half the size of the Green's. The Green is more than twice as long, the Grand being only 320 miles in length. The mean annual flow of the Grand is a bit more, but this is due to the arid nature of the lands through which the Green flows. Why, then, is the Green, obviously the master stream, relegated to second place? The answer lies not in hydrology or scientific reasoning, but in state pride and chamber of commerce politics.

The Green River joins the Grand in southeastern Utah to form the Colorado River of the West.[3] That famous stream then flows on through the Grand Canyon and into the Gulf of California. The Grand rises in Grand Lake, flows through the Grand Valley, around Grand Mesa, and through the town of Grand Junction, Colorado. Around 1920, the legislators and the Chamber of Commerce of the state of Colorado were embarrassed to realize that the famous Colorado River, the namesake of their state, was nowhere to be found within its borders. To remedy this, they began to press the newly created Board of Geographic Names of the U.S. Department of the Interior to eliminate the name "Grand River" and call the stream the Colorado along its entire length. The

Board had been created to make some sense out of the many names that were appearing on maps of the U.S., and usually they stuck with the accepted local usage in assigning an official name to any geographic feature. In this case, the profusion of Grand Lakes and Grand Valleys and so on and the persistence of the Colorado partisans made them ignore the long-established name and agree to the change. The Utah legislature went along and by act of Congress in 1922, the change became law. Considering the entire length of the Colorado from Grand Lake to the Gulf of California, the Green is indeed a tributary, but this is hardly fair. It could just as well be said that the river should be named the Green, with the Colorado as a tributary.[4]

The Green has gone by many names in the past, as different ones were used during different periods in the history of the river. What the earliest inhabitants of the river basin called the Green will never be known. The Frémont people and their ancestors lived near the river and ate the fish, waterfowl, and other animals they caught in and along the river (and no doubt knew the Green simply as the River). The later Crows and Shoshones who lived near its headwaters called it *Seeds-ke-dee Agie*, or Prairie Hen River.[5] Farther downstream the Utes called it the Bitterroot.[6] The first white men to see the upper Green, the Franciscan friars Dominguez and Escalante, called it the San Buenaventura. Spaniards who had crossed the Green on the Old Spanish Trail were familiar with its lower course, but when the Franciscans encountered the river upstream, on the other side of the Tavaputs Plateau, they believed it to be undiscovered and gave it a new name. Dominguez and Escalante reached the river in September 1776, in the middle of their ill-fated exploration of the Great Basin. Seeking a new route to California, they became lost in southwestern Utah and finally returned to Santa Fe, their expedition somewhat of a failure. Father Escalante, however, the journal-keeper for the expedition, recorded the first written description of the river when they reached its banks on 13 September 1776:

> [We] came to a large river which we named San Buenaventura . . . the most copious one we have come by. Its course along here is to the west-southwest but, ahead and down to here, to the west. Here it has a meadow abounding in pasturage and good land for farming with the help of irrigation. . . . [T]he river flows into it between two lofty stone hogbacks which, after forming a sort of corral, come so closely together that one can barely make out the gorge through which the river comes [the mouth of Split Mountain Canyon]. According to our guide, one cannot cross anywhere

else than by the single ford it has in this vicinity, which lies on the side west of the hogback on the north, very near to a chain of small bluffs of loose dirt, some lead colored and others of a yellow hue.[7]

About fifty years later, General William Ashley led a band of fur trappers down the Green. They knew the river by a variety of names, the most common being "Shetskedee" or some other corruption of the Shoshone name. Ashley does mention that he believed the river to be the Spanish River, or the Colorado of the West.[8] The real origin of the name Green River is not known. Some postulate that it was named for some member of Ashley's band of trappers. John C. Frémont, who explored the region in the 1840s, thought it was because of the vegetation that grew along its banks, giving it a green appearance in contrast to the surrounding arid badlands. Perhaps it was the color of the water, although in this case Prairie Hen River would be more appropriate. All that is known for sure is that in the Uinta Basin, Ashley met a group of trappers from Taos and learned from them that the river was commonly called Rio Verde—Green River.[9]

The origins of the names of virtually all of the rapids, canyons, and most geographical features are much more easily established. When John Wesley Powell made the first official explorations of the river in 1869 and in 1871, he exercised "explorer's right" and named everything in sight. This accounts for the romantic names some features bear, such as the Cliff of the Harp in Lodore, named because Powell observed the constellation Lyra just above the cliff one night. There are a few exceptions, but for the most part the names of geographic features along this stretch of river, and indeed along most of the Colorado River, were named by Major Powell.

The Green cuts through many canyons and meanders through a number of open areas, or bottoms, on its southward course, but it was only on one particular stretch of river that river running as we know it today got its start. Why it began on the three hundred miles from Green River, Wyoming, to the Uinta Basin is hard to say. Perhaps it was because it was easy to get to. The Oregon Trail, and later the transcontinental railroad, crossed the river north of the Uinta Mountains. For whatever reason, the fact remains that modern river running had its origins on the Green River. The Green flows through seven canyons and four large

Whirlpool Canyon.

open areas, or parks, as they are known, along this stretch. Each has its own characteristics, its own rapids, its own dangers, its own beauties.

In the sixty miles from the town of Green River, Wyoming, to Flaming Gorge, the first of the canyons, the river flowed through mostly arid clay hills.[10] Today the bottoms of these canyons, and indeed the whole river valley to within six miles of the town of Green River, are flooded by Flaming Gorge Reservoir. It is at Flaming Gorge that the canyons begin. The name comes from the brilliant red of the rocks which form the mountain's core. Next come two more short canyons in quick succession—Horseshoe Canyon and Kingfisher Canyon. Horseshoe is no more than a long bend around Beehive Point. Kingfisher was named by Powell for the abundance of birds of that type. The mouth of Sheep Creek divided the two canyons. Together these three canyons were not more than six miles long. In none of them was there anything that could be called a rapid. The water was swift, and an occasional rock broke the surface, but there was no obstacle that posed any danger to a boat even in the hands of a novice.

Red Canyon was named for its deep red Precambrian walls. In this canyon was Ashley Falls, named for the inscription left by the General, a swift drop among house-sized boulders. The rapid was much feared by early river runners, but from all accounts it was easier than it looked. Flaming Gorge Dam was built about two miles downstream from the falls, and so the rapid, as well as the historic "river register" of carvings and inscriptions of early travelers, are gone.

The remaining fifteen miles of Red Canyon below Flaming Gorge Dam are very popular with fishermen, campers, and whitewater enthusiasts. Below the dam the river runs clear and cold, seemingly an ideal habitat for trout. A trail follows the north side of the river to Little Hole, the only opening of any size in Red Canyon. The U.S. Forest Service has a campground here, and a good road leads back to Flaming Gorge Dam. In this stretch, which has become the most heavily used part of the entire river, are many small splashy rapids but the only named one is Red Creek, about two miles above the end of the canyon. It was formed by boulders washed out of Red Creek into the river during heavy rains. At any water level, Red Creek is tricky to run. It was the scene of many anxious moments for early river runners.

The river emerges from the swift water of Red Canyon into Browns Park. Here the river slows and meanders easily for about forty miles. The valley is bounded on the north and south by steep mountain slopes rising about two thousand feet above the floor. The river is lined with cottonwoods and willows, and the many marshes on either side are home to thousands of waterfowl. Originally called Brown's Hole by the Anglos, it was known as O-wi-yu-kuts (Big Valley) to the Indians who wintered there. Brown's Hole is one of the few names along the Green that didn't originate with Powell. Instead, it was named for Baptiste, or Bibleback, Brown, a trapper who lived there in the 1830s. The Mormons used the valley to winter the herds of oxen that pulled their wagons west during the great migrations to the Salt Lake Valley. They were soon followed by ranchers who fattened their cattle on the rich grass of the valley floor. Toward the end of the nineteenth century, outlaws—notably the Wild Bunch, which included Butch Cassidy and the Sundance Kid, although there were others—moved into the valley and used it as a hideout and retreat because of its inaccessibility.

At the lower end of Browns Park the river turns south and enters the Gates of Lodore, one of the most imposing canyon entrances to be found on any river. The Green quickly makes up for its lazy curves in the mad, turbulent waters of the Canyon of Lodore. Here the river disregards geology and cuts through the heart of the mountain range. The towering red walls are of the same rock as Red Canyon, but there the resemblance ends. Lodore is much deeper—over two thousand feet deep—and runs north to south, so the sun shines into the canyon for only a few hours each day. Combined with the roar of the almost continuous rapids along its eighteen miles, this produces a gloomy, overpowering feeling that profoundly affected the first explorers. For all its gloominess, though, Lodore is a darkly beautiful place, the red cliffs and buttresses accented by groves of cottonwoods and willows, and lovely side streams with such pleasing names as Rippling Brook, Alcove Brook, and Winnie's Grotto.

Except for Red Creek Rapid, Lodore is the first place that river travelers encounter any real rapids. The first of these is Winnie's Rapid, formed by a boulder fan from Winnie's Grotto on the right side of the river. It was known briefly as Loper Falls, after Bert Loper, the head boatman on the 1922 U.S. Geological Survey river expedition, but the older name won out. Winnie's is not considered one of the more difficult rapids in Lodore, but boats have been lost there. Next, and most famous of Lodore's rapids is Disaster Falls, which is actually two rapids. It was on the lower section that one of Powell's boats was wrecked, giving the rapid its name. The river drops sharply and runs along the cliff on the right side of the channel. The first part, Upper Disaster Falls, contains large waves caused by the drop and the narrow channel. If a boatman loses control in the upper waves, there is almost no way to avoid the head of the rocky island that marks the beginning of Lower Disaster Falls, where many boats have come to grief. After passing the island, the river sweeps under an overhanging cliff. Most early river travelers ran the upper part and portaged or lined the lower section. Numerous small rapids are encountered in the next two miles down to Harp Falls, just under the Cliff of the Harp, which is just a large rock in the middle of the river. Two miles farther is Triplet Falls, actually a series of three separate rapids that form an s-curve. Finally there is Hell's Half Mile, the longest and most difficult of Lodore's cataracts. It is also the best known. Once Hell's Half Mile is passed, boatmen breathe a sigh of relief and run the last few little rapids before Echo Park. Lodore was the scene of many early disasters and near-disasters, and the legends about its dangers died hard—and many are not quite dead, in fact. Now that the river is controlled by Flaming Gorge Dam, it has lost some of its fearsome character, and the rapids have been over-shadowed by the Big Drop of Cataract and those in the Grand Canyon, but they are still to be reckoned with.

Lodore ends at Echo Park, where the Yampa joins the Green. Echo Park is a hauntingly, almost painfully beautiful place, a sandstone Yosemite. Warm sandstone walls provide a welcome contrast to the gloom of Lodore. Box elder and cottonwood trees offer shade for the traveler and are home to many kinds of birds which sweeten the days with their songs. The most prominent feature of Echo Park is Steamboat Rock on the west side of the river. A seven-hundred-foot wall of sandstone that rises from the river's edge, the clear echoes that bounce from it have given the park its name. Echo Park is still known locally as Pat's Hole, after a hermit who lived there during the last part of the nineteenth century.

"The Green is greatly increased by the Yampa, and we now have a much larger river. All this volume of water, confined, as it is, in a narrow channel . . . is set eddying and spinning in whirlpools. . . . [T]he waters waltz their way through the canyon, making their own rippling, rushing, roaring music."[11] So Major Powell described the next canyon, which he named Whirlpool, in 1869. Whirlpool is about ten miles long, and is actually deeper than Lodore—almost three thousand feet—but the walls are not as steep. It can seem no less gloomy at times, but there are no Disaster Falls or Hell's Half Mile to add the element of real danger. Whirlpool's rapids—like Greasy Pliers and Dead Wombat Falls—were named by modern boatmen. Even at high water, the rapids are no more than an exhilarating ride on roller coaster waves.[12] The whirlpools, for which the canyon is aptly named, are so powerful in the spring that they can stop a fully loaded raft or flip an unsuspecting kayaker in an instant. Halfway through Whirlpool, Jones Hole Creek

Island Park with the mouth of Whirlpool Canyon in the distance.

Rainbow Park.

enters from the north, a lovely, clear stream fed by springs about five miles up its narrow gorge. It is home to a thriving population of trout, replenished by a fish hatchery built over the springs. The alluvial fan at the mouth of the creek is covered with groves of trees and has long been a favorite spot for Indians, fishermen, and river runners.

From Whirlpool, the river flows abruptly into Island Park, and once again curves lazily, meandering around islands covered with groves of cottonwoods. The openness and sweeping vistas of Island Park come as a welcome relief after days spent in the confined canyons above. A low ridge separates Island Park from Rainbow Park, named for the multicolored layers of clay and shale of the Morrison Formation seen on the north side of the river. The famous dinosaur quarry is located in a similar outcropping of the Morrison Formation on the other side of Split Mountain.

Split Mountain is another example of the Green ignoring the rules of geology. Instead of taking the easier course through the low country on the west side of the mountain, the river has taken the direct course straight down its length, creating a seven-mile canyon with four major rapids and numerous smaller ones. The name was in doubt for a while— Major Powell considered naming it Craggy Canyon for the many spires of sandstone that line the walls, but he finally concluded that the geological phenomenon was more impressive and called it by its present name. It has the sharpest drop of any of the canyons on the Green, 20.7 feet per mile.[13] Split Mountain is another canyon whose rapids were named by boatmen other than Powell's. The first is Moonshine, named after Moonshine Draw on the east side of the river, where during Prohibition someone from Vernal operated an illegal still. Moonshine is the most difficult of the rapids in Split Mountain, because of the sharp drop and the cliff along the right side. A boatman in trouble in Moonshine has less than a quarter of a mile to get ready for S.O.B., the next rapid. It was named for obvious reasons by Bus Hatch, a pioneer commercial boatman. The rapid consists of a sharp drop, followed by a quick turn to the right up against an overhanging cliff. The course of the rapid is so strewn with boulders that there is almost no clean run of S.O.B.—hence the name. Another quarter-mile brings the boatman to Schoolboy, also named by Bus Hatch. Schoolboy seems like it should be hard to run, but it is very forgiving. It is called Schoolboy because it is so easy to run that even a schoolboy could handle it.

There are some other small rapids in Split Mountain, but the last named one is Inglesby, no more than a large rock in the middle of the river. It got its name from a retired dentist from Fruita, Utah, who was foresighted enough to get thrown from a boat while running the waves below the rock and so have his name enshrined on the map of the river. Soon after Inglesby, the river makes a sweeping turn to the left and Split Mountain abruptly ends. The river is not again confined by canyon walls until it reaches Desolation Canyon, more than a hundred miles downstream. The Green wanders through the Uinta Basin, a broad, generally arid valley drained by the White River, the Duchesne River, and many small tributaries. About eighteen miles below the Park Service boat ramp at the mouth of Split Mountain Canyon is the small town of Jensen, where U.S. Highway 40 crosses the river. Jensen is the last town of any size, until Green River, Utah, some 180 miles downstream.

Today the river canyons, those that are not under Flaming Gorge Reservoir, are known, photographed, and mapped. Thousands of modern river runners and boaters are attracted by their beauties and dangers each year. It was not always so, however. In the first quarter of the nineteenth century, when the most of America seemed on the move westward, the canyons of the Green were just another unknown in a whole continent of mysteries.

Down the Seeds-ke-dee

The Dominguez-Escalante party camped by the Green River for only two days, crossed it without much comment, and then went on their way. The names of these two Franciscans are forever linked with the history of the Green, however, because they were the first non-Indians to see the river and leave a record, gave the river the name San Buenaventura, and recorded its course, however incorrectly, on a widely circulated map. Don Miera y Pacheco, the official mapmaker for the expedition, confused the Green with the Sevier River, which the Spaniards encountered later in their travels. Unaware that the Green swings to the south, Miera showed it on his map as flowing due west into the modestly named Laguna de Miera. Alexander von Humboldt, the famous German explorer and naturalist, apparently had access to a copy of Miera's map, and perpetuated the mistake on a map he made of the Spanish dominions in 1811.[1] Later generations of cartographers simply interpolated, and thus was born the mythical San Buenaventura. Even though the mountain men had known since 1826 that there was no river flowing across the Great Basin, the legend died hard. The Bartleson-Bidwell party, which emigrated from the states to California in 1841, brought along boat-building tools so that if they had to, they could make boats and float down the San Buenaventura to California.[2] The "Pathfinder," Lt. John C. Frémont, officially disproved the existence of the San Buenaventura by his explorations of the Great Basin in the early 1840s, but there were still those who chose to believe in the legend.

Such legends were current in the bustling border towns of the United States, such as St. Louis, Missouri. The energies that stirred the men in these towns were just beginning to boil over into the land so recently acquired by Thomas Jefferson. Not many years after the Franciscan friars passed through the Green River basin, Jefferson bought one-third of the future United States, the entire drainage of the Mississippi River, for the amazing sum of fifteen million dollars. Even then it was a fantastic bargain, but Napoleon had just stolen the lands from Spain and needed cash to finance his conquest of Europe. Freed by the lifting of foreign borders, restless Americans ignored their own government's attempts to restrict entry into the new lands and began to filter across the Missouri. The restless, the ambitious, the pious; drifters, explorers, missionaries, all began to move west.

Among those motivated by dreams of the riches to be made in the western lands were men who coveted the skins of an inoffensive member of the rodent family called the beaver. Tall hats of felt made from beaver fur were the rage in the fashionable circles of Europe, and some men recognized that here was a way to make huge profits at relatively little cost. The valley and the tributaries of the Green River were central to the early history of the fur trade. Some of the most colorful men in the trade camped and hunted along its banks; some of the adventures they had became the legends of the mountain men, told around many a lodge fire on many a cold winter night.

By the 1820s, the fur trade business was growing enough to draw the attention of men who recognized the quick profits to be made. One of these was a Virginia-born aspiring politician named William Ashley. He possessed a shrewd business sense, having built a powder mill near St. Louis just in time to supply the government's needs during the War of 1812.[3] Casting about for another line of business to finance his desired career in public office, he decided upon the fur trade. Ashley found the perfect partner for such a venture in another resident of St. Louis, Andrew Henry. Henry had been one of the original members of the old Missouri Fur Company and had been involved in the fur trade since 1810. He was to be the man in the field, coordinating the trapping parties and the trade with the Indians. Ashley, as befitted a man of credit, was to be the agent in St. Louis, where he would recruit trappers, outfit the field parties, and dispose of the fur harvest.

General Ashley, a brigadier general in the state militia, ran an advertisement in the 13 February 1822 issue of the *Missourie Gazette and Public Advertiser*:

TO
Enterprising young men

The subscriber wishes to engage ONE HUNDRED MEN, to ascend the river Missouri to its source, there to be employed for one, two or three years. For particulars enquire of Major Andrew Henry, near the Lead Mines, in the County of Washington, (who will ascend with, and command the party), or to the subscriber at St. Louis.

Wm. H. Ashley[4]

The "enterprising young men" who answered the ad formed the core of the fur trade, became the booshways, brigade leaders, and partisans who led the trapping parties until the trade finally dried up in the 1840s. Their names read like a hall of fame of the mountain men: William Sublette, Tom Fitzpatrick, Jim Beckwourth, Jim Bridger, James Clyman, Black Harris, Hugh Glass. Others soon joined Ashley's company. Some became famous, like Joe Meek and Kit Carson; others were not so famous, but because they knew how to write, they kept diaries that have left a record of the life of mountain men.

For all this stellar crew, however, Ashley and Henry got off to a bad start. Their first two years saw their parties ambushed and murdered by Indians, and the loss of a keel boat with a whole year's outfit. At that point, Henry decided he had had enough, and quit the mountains altogether.[5] Ashley was left to carry on alone, so he decided to abandon the Missouri as a route to the West. With a pack train, he headed overland to strike what was then variously known as the Spanish River, the Colorado of the West, or among the trappers themselves, the Seedske-dee. In doing so, he revolutionized the fur trade.

Before going into Ashley's adventures on the river, however, it should be mentioned that his was not the first party of trappers to see the upper Green. The Snake Country Expeditions of the Hudson's Bay Company under Alexander MacKenzie had trapped there during the 1820-21 season. Ashley's lieutenant, Jedediah Smith, had also trapped

along the banks of the Green in 1824, but it was left for the General
to be the first to travel down the river itself.[6]

Ashley and his men reached the Green on Sunday, 9 April 1825.
He recorded the event laconically: "[We] traveled west 6 miles over
a broken sandy country and came to the Shetskeedee."[7] Another member
of the General's party, the mulatto Jim Beckwourth, described the same
scene a bit differently:

> I discovered a river which I had never seen in this region before. It was
> of considerable size, flowing four or five miles distant. . . . I hailed this
> as a perfect godsend, and was overjoyed with the feeling of security in-
> fused by my opportune discovery. . . . We all arrived in good season on
> the banks of Green River.[8]

Beckwourth goes on to say that his companions had already killed a
"fine buffalo" from one of the large herds he had observed while dis-
covering the river. Actually, as Ashley recorded, their supper that night
was considerably less sumptuous than fine buffalo:

> Monday 20th . . . the men . . . have been for the last two days without
> any thing to eat and they are becoming quite uneasy under the privation.
> One of the hunters brought in a horse which he found running at large
> on the river bottoms.[9]

Fine buffalo it wasn't, but horse meat was better than no meat at all.
Camped on the banks of the Green, Ashley decided to combine exploring with trapping, as a good knowledge of the country was essential to a successful hunt. He split his party into four groups. One, under
Zachariah Ham, went west; Fitzpatrick led a party south, along the river;
and James Clyman was sent north. With the remaining seven men, the
General proposed to explore the river itself by boat. The craft Ashley
chose for this undertaking was a bullboat, which the mountain men had
adopted from the Indians for navigating the streams and rivers of the
West. They were built of fresh buffalo hides stretched over a frame-
work of willow branches. The result was probably a bit unwieldy, and
they could only be used for a short time before they became waterlogged
and had to be abandoned, but they served Ashley's purpose nicely.

Before separating the party, Ashley had an idea that in hindsight
turns out to be nothing less than inspiration. This marching back and
forth by the whole party from St. Louis to the mountains was expensive, he realized. Instead, he would have all his trapping parties meet
at a designated rendezvous to receive their supplies for the year and

turn over their catch of furs. That way the brigades could winter in the mountains and get a jump on the spring's hunt. In turn, Ashley could spend most of the year in St. Louis, with its more civilized attractions. He gave the following instructions to his men:

> I will transport the goods and extra baggage down the river to some conspicious point. . . . The deposite will be made on or near the river. . . . The deposite as aforesaid will be the place of rendavose.[10]

Thus was initiated that most famous institution of the mountain men, the rendezvous. This combination business convention, sporting competition, reunion, and bacchanal went on sometimes for weeks, and was held every year save one until 1840. Most of them were held on the banks of the Green River. If the mountain men are still remembered for anything, it is for the rendezvous.

Gear and extra baggage all loaded, trapping parties dispatched, Ashley and his crew set off down the river. The river travelers soon found that one bullboat was too small for their load, so they stopped and built another. On Sunday 3 May, Ashley found a suitable place for a rendezvous and cached his goods, calling the place Rendavose Creek. This picturesque name did not, unfortunately, survive the era of the mountain men, and it is now known as Henry's Fork. Up to this point, the explorers had found the navigation of the river to be unobstructed. Immediately below the cache, however, this changed. The current quickened, the canyon narrowed, and the men began to feel the first faint stirrings of unease.

The first three canyons, Flaming Gorge, Horseshoe, and Kingfisher, were passed without any serious difficulties. The current was swift, and there were exposed rocks, but no real rapids. Next, however, they entered Red Canyon, and almost immediately came upon the first of the many obstructions choking the bottom of the canyon. Later that same afternoon, they came upon their first real rapid:

> [T]he roaring and agitated state of the water a short distance before us indicated a fall or some other obstruction of considerable magnitude. . . .
> It proved to be a perpendicular fall of ten or twelve feet produced by large fragments of rocks which had fallen from the [mountain] and settled in the river extending entirely across its channel and forming an impregnable barrier to the passage of loaded watercraft. We were therefore obliged to unload our boats of their cargoes and pass them empty over the falls by means of long cords which we had provided for such purposes.[11]

Red Canyon.

The rapid was after known as Ashley Falls. While his men were portaging and lining the boats, the General climbed to a cliff above the river and painted ASHLEY 1825 in large black letters, which was noticed by John Wesley Powell some forty-five years later.[12] Ashley and his men continued deeper into the canyon country. Finally, on the fifth of May, the trappers reached Browns Park, and the weary men were afforded a respite from the labor of portaging and lining their boats and baggage. The mountaineers were to need this breathing spell, for as Dale Morgan says, "Ashley was plunging headlong into a kind of country nothing in the American experience had prepared him for,"[13] the dark and gloomy Canyon of Lodore.

Ashley and his men quickly encountered a succession of rapids upon entering the canyon. The labor and stress of maneuvering their unwieldy boats through this maelstrom of boulders and rushing water quickly began to show on the men. Ashley spoke for all of them on 8 May:

> As we passed along between these massy walls, which in great degree exclude from us the rays of heaven, I was forcibly struck by the gloom which spread over the countenances of my men; they seemed to anticipate (and not too far distant, too) a dreadful termination of our voyage, and I must confess that I partook in some degree of their feelings, for things around us truly had an awful appearance.[14]

After about four days of hard work at the foot of somber canyon walls, the men reached Echo Park, where the Yampa meets the Green. Ashley called the Yampa Mary's River; his men would come to know it as Bear River. He went on to describe Whirlpool Canyon, Island Park, and Split Mountain Canyon. In the latter gorge, the voyagers had their first real mishap. Ashley, anxious to get downriver, kept the boats in the water a little too long, and was unable to get to shore in time to avoid a rapid:

> [S]oon after entering the heavy billows our boat filled with water but did not sink. . . . [T]wo of the most active men then leaped in the water took the cables and towed her to land just as from all appearances she was making her exit and me with her for I cannot swim and my only hope was that the boat would not sink.[15]

Another version of this same incident was told by James Beckwourth. Never mind that Beckwourth was at the time on the other side of the Uintas with James Clyman. Like most mountain men, Beckwourth was never one to let facts get in the way of a good story. In his memoirs, written in a California gold camp in the 1850s, Beckwourth breathlessly related how he rescued General Ashley from the dreaded Green River Suck. Before that, however, he gave a description, "in as concise a manner as possible," of the Suck itself:

> The current . . . became exceedingly rapid, and drew toward the centre from each shore. This place we named the Suck. This fall continued for

six or eight miles, making a sheer descent, in the entire distance, of up-
ward of two hundred and fifty feet.

Jim goes on to say that when the General unwisely jumped into one
of their newly constructed boats to test it, the rope holding it to the
shore broke. The boat drifted into the Suck, capsized, and Ashley was
thrown into the current. He made it to the opposite shore, "as Provi-
dence would have it," and called for help. Beckwourth plunged into
the icy current, swam over to the hapless general, and directed him
to hold onto his shoulders and kick out when told to:

> We swam to within a few yards of the opposite shore, where the main
> suck caught us, and, my strength becoming exhausted we began slowly
> to recede from the shore toward inevitable death. At this moment Fitz-
> patrick thrust a long pole toward us, to the end of which he attached a
> rope which the party on shore retained possession of. I seized the pole
> with a death-grip, and we were hauled out of our perilous situation; a
> few moment's delay, and the world had seen the last of us. After this res-
> cue, the general remarked to Fitzpatrick, "That Beckwourth is surely one
> of the most singular men I ever met."[16]

Soon after this adventure, Ashley and his men were no doubt glad
to leave the perils of the canyons and enter the Uinta Basin. There were
no more canyons as far as they could see, and that probably suited them.
By the sixteenth of the month, Ashley was camped at the mouth of the
stream that still carries his name. Here he met two men from a party
of trappers let by Etienne Provost. This group had followed the old
Indian route north from Taos, New Mexico, over the Book Cliffs and
into the Uinta Basin by way of Willow Creek. Ashley asked them about
the nature of the country downstream, but didn't get a very encouraging answer. Four of their men had tried to descend the river and had
encountered only hostile Indians and no game. The trappers were, in
fact, reduced to eating the skins of the beaver they had caught. Ashley,
after caching his goods, floated down the Green to the mouth of the
White River. At this favorite wintering place for the Taos trappers, he
found Provost's camp but no Provost. Ashley still wanted to see for
himself what lay downstream, so he split his party again, sending three
of them out hunting. With the remaining three, he continued down the
Green. He was looking for Indians from whom he could buy horses,
but it was not until three days later, on the twenty-sixth, that Ashley
finally met some Utes. The country he had found to be "a barren heap
of rocky mountains." The Indians, however, were more impressive:

"These people were well dressed and treated us in the most friendly and respectful manner. . . . Their horses were better than Indian horses generally are."[17] From these sartorially pleasing natives, Ashley was able to buy a few horses—not as many as he would have liked, but enough to get his goods back to the rendezvous.

After this, Ashley and his men, in company with Provost and his men, traveled west to the Great Salt Lake and on to the rendezvous. William Ashley stayed on in the fur trade for a few more years, although 1825 was his only year in the mountains. He was able to amass a considerable fortune and finally gave up the fur trade for his first love, politics. He still kept his hand in, keeping in touch with those actively involved in the trade and lobbying in Congress for the interests of the fur business. It seems somehow fitting that Ashley's death in 1838 coincided with the decline of the fur trade. For someone who didn't really want to be in the mountains in the first place, Ashley looms large in the history of the mountain men. The list of accomplishments by him and his lieutenants is impressive: first to abandon the Missouri River route and strike overland; first to cross South Pass going west; first to explore the Green by boat; and, of course, the first to hold a rendezvous. Perhaps Ashley's greatest contribution to the fur trade, however, was the men he brought into the business. They crop up no matter what aspect of the fur trade, or exploration and settlement of the west, is studied. Along with the gambler, the emigrant, the cowboy and the Indian, and the cavalry-to-the-rescue, these colorful figures have taken their place in the gallery of western American stereotypes. It is ironic that these men, who went to the mountains to escape the public gaze, should have been so enshrined.

History has left us an interesting footnote to General Ashley's story. The valley in which his river journey came to an end is today called Ashley Valley, and through it flows Ashley Creek. Little was known of either Ashley or his exploits a scant forty-five years after his river voyage. Powell makes no mention of Ashley Valley or Ashley Creek in 1869, and yet the first Mormon settlers, who arrived ten years later, knew both. Since Ashley was long dead by that time, and his deeds apparently forgotten, how did the name get passed along? Could one of his men have come back later to trap or even to settle in the valley? It would be just the type of place that would attract a mountain man: well watered, with game, grass, and shelter. Uncle Jack Robinson, another mountain man, was attracted by the country around Henry's Fork,

on the other side of the Uintas, and came back to settle there when he
got old. Even though the first Mormon settlers left no record of how
the name originated, it is not impossible that the Saints encountered
an aging mountain man, or Indian, for that matter, who remembered
the Ashley days and passed along the name.

Just a few years after Ashley's voyage, another mountain man was
on the river, and navigating it with much more success than the General.
Denis Julien was a trapper and trader who probably came up from Taos.
His background, his life, and the date of his death are unknown, but
that in itself does not make him any different than hundreds of men
who went west during the same period and were never heard from again.
What sets him apart from other trappers is that he was apparently as
much at home in the bottoms of the canyons of the Green and the
Colorado as any trapper was in a skin lodge in the mountains.

Julien, like Ashley before him, was one to leave his name on canyon walls. Sometimes it was his full name, sometimes just his initials
and the date. At least once he embellished it with drawings and sym-
bols, such as the inscription at Hell Roaring Canyon on the lower Green.
He left other inscriptions in Desolation Canyon, Cataract Canyon, on
Inscription Rock near Whiterocks, Utah, and in Whirlpool Canyon.

What little is known about Julien's background is typical of the men
of the period. He was probably born sometime in the 1770s; by 1800
or so he was on the frontier, trading with the Indians for Pierre Choteau.
By 1827, he was west of the Rockies, working for one of the Robidoux
brothers out of Taos. In 1831, the date of the earliest known inscription, when he would have been nearly sixty years old, he and Auguste
Archambeau established a post on the Uinta River near Whiterocks.
By that time the number of beaver on the streams around the Green
was dwindling, so like many others, Julien began searching for new
trapping grounds. He chose to look for beaver along the banks of the
Green River.

Julien's inscriptions have left a chronology of his travel in the
canyons. In 1831, he was near Whiterocks; in 1836, in Labyrinth and
Cataract canyons, near the confluence of the Green and the Colorado.
Legend had it for years that Julien drowned in the treacherous waters
of Cataract Canyon. It makes a good story, but an inscription by Julien
in Whirlpool Canyon dated 1838, which was found by a park ranger

from Dinosaur National Monument, proves otherwise.[18] In the end it does not matter very much how he died. Many trappers went to a lonely death; Indians, grizzlies, exposure, and starvation were occupational hazards. It would be nice to think that Julien floated other rivers searching for beaver, and finally "went under" peacefully, in his lodge with his Indian wife nearby.[19]

Julien was not the only mountain man to explore the river canyons, although he was the only one to make it look easy. One of the others was Joe Meek. In the winter of 1839, Meek and some companions set out from Ft. Davy Crockett, a trading post at the lower end of Browns Park, seeking adventures.

> On one of these excursions Meek went with a party down the canyon of the Green River, on the ice. For nearly a hundred miles they traveled down this awful canyon without finding but one place where they could have come out; and left it at last at the mouth of the Uintee.[20]

The next spring, Ft. Davy Crockett, which had only been built a few years before, was abandoned. The men there began to split up into small parties and head for more favorable climes. One group set off for Ft. Hall, where the Hudson's Bay Company had a trading post; another headed for the South Platte River and the states. Yet another, led by Joe Walker, decided on a different course. "There is a party going in boats from this valley [Browns Park] in the Spring, down Grand River or the Colorado River of the West, to California. They will be led by Mr. Walker, who was with Bonneville in the mountains. They intend trapping for Beaver on the way."[21]

There is no existing record of the attempt. Walker must have heard about Meek's trip down the ice, and so would have had a good idea of what sort of difficulties such a trip would entail. He could have even discussed the venture with Denis Julien, who was probably a visitor at the fort. If Walker did try the river route, he would have had the same experience that Ashley had had fifteen years earlier. At any rate, Walker and a companion did show up in California the next spring, but the packs of beaver they had were carried on horseback, not in bull-boats.[22]

Another persistent rumor that was heard about the river canyons whenever groups of trappers got together and started swapping stories

Browns Park.

concerned a pair of Spanish friars and their Indian servants. According to the tale, against the advice of the Indians these two tried to navigate the river all the way to California. Their boat upset in Lodore and the two padres were drowned.[23] Whether this is a true story or not is of little import here. The significance is that even though Ashley and Julien had been down the river and thereby proved that it could be run, the canyons were still considered to be places not fit for any man, places still of mystery and legend.

By the middle of the 1840s, the fur trade was dead, killed by a capricious shift in men's fashions and a decimated beaver population. Beaver hats fell out of fashion; silk hats became the proper thing for a gentleman to wear. Times were changing along the river as well. Many of the mountain men were either ''gone beaver''—dead—or left to ''float their stick'' elsewhere. Some went on to California and Oregon; others went back to the states, and still others turned to guiding parties of emigrants or soldiers into the wilderness. In 1844, two parties which were in their different way signs of the changing times, showed up in Browns Park.

The first was a group led by Andrew Sublette. Andy was the younger brother of Milton and William Sublette, both of whom had started out in the trade in the Ashley days. The group the younger Sublette was guiding was composed not of trappers or even emigrants, but of invalids from Missouri who had heard of the mild climate in Browns Park and hoped that spending a season there would restore their health. They left Independence, Missouri, in May, and by August had reached the Green River. Whether the ''cure'' worked or not we have unfortunately no way of knowing; there is no further record of what became of them. Jim Clyman, another former Ashley man, mentioned in his memoirs that three of them had died on the way to Browns Park. Perhaps the rest found the sheltered valley by the Green a more healthful place than the open prairie.[24]

In June of 1844, while Sublette and his charges were still on their way to Browns Park, the valley was visited briefly by another party. Brevet Captain John C. Frémont, U.S. Army Corps of Topographical Engineers, came into the park on 6 June on the homeward leg of his second successful survey of the interior West. Guided by the veteran mountain man Kit Carson, the expedition camped on the south side of the river, across from the ruins of Ft. Davy Crockett. It is easy to imagine Carson regaling the wide-eyed soldiers with tales of more exciting times in the park. The pathfinder himself, however, was apparently not much impressed. All Frémont recorded in his *Report* was that after crossing the river in an old skin boat, they camped ''opposite to the remains of an old fort on the left bank of the river.''[25]

Frémont's report was read by many of those planning to take the long road west. The Mormons, planning their mass migration at Winter Quarters during the winter of 1846-47, and the emigrant companies heading for the new lands of the Oregon Territory, closely studied his descriptions of the routes to their respective promised lands. Historians generally give Frémont credit for finally laying to rest the myth of a water route to California. To generations of Americans used to traveling on the broad rivers of the east, however, the idea of floating to the new gold fields was not so easily given up. For some men, the Buenaventura was still very much a reality.

3

If We Had a Boat

Camped by the side of the Green River in August 1843, Captain Frémont had time to reflect on what he had heard about its course:

> [It] is but little known, and that little derived from vague report. Three hundred miles of its lower part, as it approaches the Gulf of California, is reported to be smooth and tranquil; but its upper part is manifestly broken into many falls and rapids. From many descriptions of trappers, it is probable that in its foaming course among its lofty precipices it presents many scenes of wild grandeur; and though offering many temptations, and often discussed, no trappers have been found bold enough to undertake a voyage which has so certain a prospect of a fatal termination.[1]

By the end of the decade, not much more was known about the river than he stated in his report. Frémont did prove that there was no river that went straight west from the vicinity of the Great Salt Lake, but the mountain men had known that as early as Jed Smith's journey across Nevada and western Utah in 1826. No one knew, however, just exactly where the river *did* go. It took a stronger motivation than beaver skins to lure the next voyagers down the river. The next time someone tried the "voyage [with] so certain a prospect of a fatal termination," it was gold, not beaver fur, that drove them on.

The news spread like an epidemic across America: gold had been discovered in California! And so they went; in droves they deserted the farms, the shops, the cities. Ships were left to swing at anchor in the harbors. Troops deserted their posts. The crops and the chickens went untended. Sweethearts were left to pine away while their beaus went off to try their luck in the gold fields. The population of Oregon, the promised land for an earlier generation of emigrants, declined so rapidly that Congress began to reconsider granting it statehood. The gold seekers, "argonauts" in the phrase of the times, went by ship around Cape Horn or across the Isthmus of Panama, or they crossed the prairies and the rugged Sierra Nevada by foot, on horseback, or by ox train.

Among the latter was a young Vermont-born Yankee named William Manly, who had already led quite an adventurous life, having left the family farm in Michigan to seek his fortune at trapping. Manly used his earnings to buy a piece of land in Wisconsin, but farming obviously wasn't in his blood. He had just about made up his mind to go to Oregon when he heard the rumors of gold in California. The "dreams at night of picking up the yellow dust" changed his mind, and he joined the throng on its way west.[2]

Manly found a man in Iowa who was leading a party to California, and hired on to drive one of his oxteams. Since Manly knew how to drive a team, the leader of the train, a Mr. Dallas, was glad to find him. They paused in St. Joseph, Missouri, long enough to buy supplies; from there, it was nothing but vast distances and a dusty trail. They had their share of adventures common to crossing the plains: swollen rivers, little or bad water, bugs, dust, cholera, Indians. When they encountered their first buffalo herds, they had to hunt the shaggy beasts. One of the other drivers, John Rodgers, with whom Manly was already good friends, got too close to the quarry. His horse suffered a gash from the buffalo's horns "while Mr. Rodgers went on a flying expedition over the horses head, and did some lively scrambling when he reached the ground."[3]

On their outward journey they met a group of Mormons, who Manly seemed to think was just about as dangerous as the buffalo. Having just come from Illinois and Missouri, he had no doubt heard plenty of stories about the Saints, and he describes one particular bunch in detail.

About this time we met an odd looking train going east, consisting of five or six Mormons from Salt Lake, all mounted on small Spanish Mules. They were dressed in buckskin and moccasins with long spurs jingling at their heels, the rowells fully four inches long, and each one carried a gun, a pistol, and a big knife. They were rough-looking fellows with long matted hair, long beards, old slouch hats and a generally backwoods get-up air in every way. They had an extra pack mule, but their baggage and provisions were very light. I had heard much about the Mormons, both at Nauvoo and Salt Lake, and some way or other I could not separate the idea of horse thieves from this party, and I am sure I would not like to meet them if I had a desirable mule that they wanted, or any money, or a good looking wife.[4]

Manly's train fell in with a troop of cavalry on their way to Oregon, and the two parties traveled together until they reached the crossing of the Green River. Manly had the opportunity to talk with the surgeon of the troopers, a well-traveled man who had been the same route before and knew something of the country they would have to cross before they got to California. He told the emigrants it was too late to cross the Sierras; they would surely come to grief just as the Donner party had only a few years before. They would be forced to winter in Salt Lake City, among the Mormons. Manly was none too thrilled with this prospect, remembering the rough-looking crew they had met back up the trail. The surgeon knew something about the Saints as well, and he filled the young man in on them. If you are forced to winter among the Mormons, the doctor warned, "do not let them know you are from Missouri. . . . [T]hey were driven from Missouri, and will get revenge if they can."[5] Good advice; even though Manly wasn't from Missouri, the others in the train were, and to the Mormons, so soon after their expulsion from that state, guilt by association was probably sufficient. As if the surgeon's warnings weren't enough bad news, Manly and the other drivers found out that Mr. Dallas couldn't afford to keep them over the winter and planned to let them go. They were to be left to fend for themselves in Salt Lake City.

Manly and the rest of the drivers began to think about alternatives. While camped on the banks of the Green, they had not failed to notice that the river was "a clear and rapid stream," with smooth sailing as far as the eye could see. These men were from places such as Ohio, Illinois, and Missouri, where travel by river had been a way of life for generations. Besides, it was fairly common knowledge that the Green came out somewhere on the Pacific Coast. No one knew just where, admittedly, but right then anything must have seemed better than spending the winter in Salt Lake City among the Saints. The predicament, the smooth river flowing by, the dangers ahead versus the dangers to be found downriver, got Manly and his compatriots to thinking:

> We put a great many "ifs" together and they amounted to about this: If this stream were large enough; if we had a boat; if we knew the way; if there were no falls or bad places; if we had plenty of provisions; if we were bold enough to start out on such a trip, etc., we might come out at some point or other on the Pacific ocean. And now when we came to the first of the "ifs," a stream large enough to float a small boat, we began to think more strongly about the other "ifs."[6]

The second "if" was quickly fulfilled, for they found an abandoned ferryboat filled with sand, and it didn't take them long to dig it out and get it ready. Two paddles were found beneath it, and the men cut some willow poles to use in pushing their craft along in the shallow parts. Things began to look up. The friendly surgeon assured them, according to Manly, that the river did indeed run all the way to the Pacific, and that they would encounter "no obstacles except cataracts, which [he] had heard were pretty bad."

Manly sold his pony to Mr. Dallas for sixty dollars, and traded for some flour and bacon. The leader was sorry to see his drivers go, but he threw in some rope and a couple of axes. After helping the emigrant train and the soldiers cross the river, Manly and the drivers parted company with the rest of the train and the troopers. Dallas and his party went on to Salt Lake City, the soldiers on to Ft. Hall and Oregon, and, as Manly noted, he and his small band were left "sitting on the bank of the river whose waters flowed to the Great Pacific."

It is easy to imagine the feelings of that small group of men as they watched the wagons creak out of sight. Had they made the right decision? They were far from the nearest settlement, in Indian country, on the bank of an unknown and maybe unnavigable river. Manly expressed it well: "All our worldly goods were piled up on the bank, and we were alone."

There was plenty to be done. First, they organized the company and elected Manly as captain, over his objections. They next took stock of their provisions and equipment: six guns for seven men, a couple of axes, a few hatchets, some flour and bacon, and a length of rope. The ferryboat was in fair shape; being buried in the sand had preserved it. It was rather clumsy, having been made to go across the river, not down it, and oddly proportioned for what they intended to do, but it was sturdy and watertight. By then they had little choice anyway: it was a long walk to Salt Lake City. They loaded themselves and their gear onto the boat and shoved off.

Spirits were high at first, as the travelers were no doubt relieved just to be doing something, going somewhere. The river was smooth and swift, the day warm, and California didn't seem so far off after all. Manly spoke for all:

> [I]t looked as if we were taking the most sensible way to get to the Pacific, and we almost wondered that everyone was so blind as not to see it as we did. . . . [W]e commenced to move down the river with ease and comfort, feeling much happier than we would had we been going toward Salt Lake with the prospect of wintering there.[7]

They passed an Indian camp at the mouth of Ham's Fork. Some of the Indians ran to the bank and beckoned for them to come ashore, but Manly didn't trust them and drifted on past. The Indians might have been trying to tell them something, for the idyllic gliding down the glassy stream soon came to an end. The Green suddenly turned into a "rapid, roaring river," and rocks began to appear in the channel. With the poles they had cut downstream, the company tried to keep the boat in the middle of the shallow channel. One time Manly set his pole and gave it a shove, but the pole stuck between two rocks. He ended up taking an unexpected swim, much to the amusement of the rest of the crew. Manly climbed back onto the boat and admonished them, a bit testily: "I told them that was nothing, as we were on our way to California by water anyway, and such things must be expected."[8] Manly had no idea just how prophetic his warning would be.

Rocks, swift current, unexpected dunkings and all, it was still better than staring at the back end of a plodding ox, breathing dust, and fighting flies. They estimated that they were making thirty miles a day; much of their time was spent taking turns sleeping and daydreaming of the riches that would be theirs once they got to California.

By the fifth day they began to near the upper canyons. Manly describes their surprise and dismay when they rounded a corner and could see that the river seemed to disappear into the mountain:

> [T]he boat came around a small angle in the stream, and all at once there seemed to be a higher, steeper range of mountains right across the valley. The boys thought the river was coming to a rather sudden end . . . and

Entrance to Flaming Gorge.

for the life of me I could not say they were not right, for there was no way in sight for it to go. I remembered while looking over a map the military men had, I found a place named Brown's Hole, and I told the boys I guessed we were elected to go on foot to California after all, for I did not propose to follow the river down any sort of hole into any mountain. We were floating directly toward a perpendicular cliff, and I could not see any hole anywhere, nor any other place where it could go.[9]

Just as they got to the cliff, though, the river made a sharp turn and went behind a high ridge. They entered a deep canyon, with walls so steep that they seemed to hang over the river. This was Flaming Gorge, the first of more than a hundred miles of canyons.

Now their real work began. Rocks became more and more frequent in the narrow channel, and they often had to get out into the cold water and push the boat off them. They saw an old cottonwood tree on the bank with the marks of an axe on it, but the only other signs of life in the gloomy canyon were the mountain sheep, which silently watched them pass from the safety of the high cliffs. At one point when they stopped to rest, Manly felt the urge to leave some sort of record of their passage, just as General Ashley had a quarter-century before:

I climbed up above the high water mark which we could clearly see, and with a mixture of gunpowder and grease for paint, and a bit of cloth tied

to a stick for a brush, I painted in fair sized letters on the rock, CAPT.
W.L. MANLY U.S.A. We did not know whether we were within the bound
of the United States or not, and we put on all the majesty we could under
the circumstances.[10]

Just downstream from this spot, they came to Ashley Falls, the rapid
where the General had left *his* mark. The forty-niners successfully
maneuvered their awkward craft around the huge boulders that blocked
the stream and camped below the rapid. Manly noticed the name on
the cliff above their camp, and recognized it from Missouri; it may have
been comforting to know that someone else besides Indians had been
there before them.

A short distance below the falls, their real troubles began, where
another big boulder blocked the channel. Trying to get their ferryboat
around the obstruction, they lost their grip and the boat wedged itself
against the upstream side of the boulder. With the strong current against
it, Manly says, "we could no more move it than we could move the
rock itself." They had fortunately unloaded all of their baggage and
gear before attempting to pass the boulder, but at the moment that seemed
small comfort, as Manly recorded: "[T]here were some very rapid
thoughts as to whether we would not be safer among the Mormons than
out in this wild country, afoot and alone."

Manly, however, was not one to let such a thing get him down for
long, and as their elected leader he could not let the men sit on the bank
of the river, staring at the lost boat, bewailing their fate. He saw some
tall pine trees nearby and concluded that dugout canoes were the answer. The men fell to work and "never let the axes rest night or day,"
until two canoes were finished, about fifteen feet long and two feet
across. Even tied together side by side, however, the men found that
there was not enough room to carry all of them. Just downstream, they
found two more pine trees, much taller than the first two, and again
the canyon resounded to the sound of axes. These two dugouts were
a little less than thirty feet long, and lashed together they made a more
stable craft than the first. Their most important gear and remaining food
was loaded in the larger boat, and the men resumed their interrupted
journey.

The swift current soon brought them out into Browns Park. Game
was abundant, and before long they had a deer, a couple of elk, and
a few ducks. The larger of the two elk was estimated to weigh five or

Manly and his crew in Red Canyon.

six hundred pounds. The antlers were so large that a man could walk upright through them. The men stayed up all night drying the meat.

Back on the river, they found signs that men other than Indians were nearby. "We saw one place where a large band of horses had crossed," Manly noted, "and as the men with them must have had a raft, we were pretty sure that the men in charge of them were white men."

It took the forty-niners about three days to float through the quiet waters of the park. All the while they were approaching the Gates of

Lodore, but perhaps their earlier experience at Flaming Gorge lulled them into false security, for Manly makes no mention of any foreboding. Their complacence was shattered, however, as soon as they entered the canyon. "The mountains seemed to change into bare rocks and get higher and higher," Manly wrote. At the same time, the river became so rough that they had to constantly unload their canoes and drag them around the boulders, carry the loads around and reload them, only to face the same task a little farther downstream.

At the rapid later identified by Major Powell as Disaster Falls, they found signs of other river travelers, this time some who had apparently preceded them into the canyons. The sight was none too encouraging, as Manly records:

> At one place where the river was more than usually obstructed we found a deserted camp, a skiff and some heavy cooking utensils, with a notice posted up on an alder tree saying that they had found the river route impracticable, and being satisfied that the river was so full of rocks and boulders that it could not be safely navigated, they had abandoned the undertaking and were about to start overland to make their way to Salt Lake. I took down the names of the parties at the time in my diary, which has since been burned, but have now forgotten them entirely. They were all strangers to me. They had left such heavy articles as could not be carried on foot. This notice rather disconcerted us, but we thought we had better keep on and see for ourselves, so we did not follow them, but kept on down the rocky river. We found generally more boulders than water.[11]

Manly and his men began to gain confidence, and ran more of the rapids, although this might have been to avoid the arduous portages. Manly, in the big canoe was always in the lead, as he was the only one who had any experience in small boats. At one particularly bad rapid, probably Triplet Falls or Hell's Half Mile, the second canoe tried to follow the leader and didn't quite make it. The boat swamped, and one of the passengers who couldn't swim saved himself. "[H]e threw up his hands and splashed and kicked at a terrible rate," Manly comments dryly. Another of the crewmen, who held onto the overturned canoe with a "death grip," almost drowned nevertheless, but was saved by the resourceful leader at the last moment. The men were frightened by their swim in the rapid, and thought they had lost all they owned. When they righted the canoe, however, they found that their clothes and blankets had floated and were saved, even though they had lost their guns and camp gear.

Soon after this rapid, they reached Echo Park. Here Manly managed
to shoot three mountain sheep, and the boys could enjoy their first good
meal since Browns Park. The fresh meat and openness of the park after Lodore's gloomy depths raised their spirits considerably, and they
"had a merry time after all." From this point on, the river canyons
were less constricted, and the rapids, though still frequent, were not
as violent. Finally, after passing Split Mountain without a comment from
Manly, they came into the Uinta Basin. The river was calm as far as
the eye could see, with cottonwoods and willows lining its banks. A
new problem soon arose, however. The barren valley seemed to be empty
of game; though the men weren't lining and portaging rapids, they were
getting hungry. They began to worry about the lack of food, but something happened that took their minds off their growling stomachs:

> We were floating along very silently one day, for none of us felt very
> much in the mood for talking, when we heard a distant sound which we
> thought was very much like the firing of a gun. . . . Again and again we
> heard it, and decided that it must be a gunshot. . . . We were pretty sure
> there were no white people ahead of us, and we did not suppose the in-
> dians in this far-off land had any fire arms. . . . If it was a hostile band
> we could not do much with a rifle and a shotgun toward defending our-
> selves or taking the agressive. Some of the boys spoke of our scalps or-
> namenting a spear handle, and indulged in such like cheerful talk which
> comforted us wonderfully. Finally we concluded we did not come out into
> that wild country to be afraid of a few gunshots, and determined to put
> on a bold front, fight if we had to, run away if we could not do any better,
> and take our chances on getting scalped or roasted.[12]

Just then they saw some lodges, and a moment later an Indian standing on the riverbank with his gun over his arm. Putting on a bold front,
they landed and followed the brave to the camp.

> [T]here we heard the first word that was at all like English and that was
> "Mormonee," with a sort of questioning tone. Pretty soon one said
> "buffalo," and then we concluded they were on a big hunt of some sort.
> They took us into their lodges and showed us blankets, knives, and guns,
> and then, with a suggestive motion, said all was "Mormonee," by which
> we understood they had got them from the Mormons. The Indian in the
> back part of the lodge looked very pleasant and his countenance showed
> a good deal of intelligence for a man of the mountains. I now told the
> boys that we were in a position where we were dependent on some one,
> and that I had seen enough to convince me that these Indians were per-
> fectly friendly with the Mormons, and that for our own benefit we had
> better pass ourselves off for Mormons, also. So we put our right hand

to our breast and said "Mormonee," with a cheerful countenance, and conveyed to them the belief that we were chosen disciples of the great and only Brigham and we became friends at once, as all acknowledged. The fine-looking Indian who sat as king in the lodge now, by motions and a word or two, made himself known as Chief Walker, and when I knew this I took great pains to cultivate his acquaintance.[13]

Wakara, or Walker, was a war chief of the Utes, and was at the height of his power. He could afford to be generous to a bunch of scraggly river travelers, and might have thought that anyone crazy enough to float down the river in a hollowed-out log should be treated with respect. Wakara was already famous, or infamous, depending on whether one spoke English or Spanish, for his raids into California. There he would steal thousands of horses and cattle from the ranchos, and drive them back to New Mexico along the Old Spanish Trail, stopping along the way to pick up a few Paiute captives. In Santa Fe and the other pueblos, the booty, both equine and human, was sold to Spanish or American buyers, neither of whom were choosy about the origins of the stock, as long as the price was right. Little wonder, then, that among the California ranchos, Wakara was known as "El Diablo."

The Mormons, with whom the Utes were so friendly, were at this time still practicing Brigham Young's Indian policy of feed them, don't fight them. This accounts for the Indian's attitude toward the Saints, and Manly's friendly reception. A few years later, when Wakara figured out that the Mormons were covetous of his lands, the Utes raided the Mormon settlements, killing a number of residents. This outbreak of violence was known as the Walker War.[14]

Back on the riverbank, it turned out that Manly knew some sign language and was able to communicate with the Utes. By now he was getting quite friendly with the great Wakara. The Mericat (American, or white) learned that they were about four days from the Mormon settlements. Manly in turn told Wakara that he was traveling to California and that he thought it but a short distance downriver. The Ute chief was amazed at Manly's ignorance, and soon disabused him of his foolish notions.

When I told Chief Walker this he seemed very much astonished, as if wondering why we were going down the river when we wanted to get west across the country. I asked him how many sleeps it was to the big water. . . . [H]e then led me down to a smooth sand bar on the river and began to make a map in the sand. First he made a long crooked mark, ten feet long or so, and point[ed] to the river to let me know that the mark in the sand was made to represent it. He then made a straight mark across near the north end of the stream, and showed the other streams which came into the Green River which I saw at once was exactly correct. . . . Then he began to describe the river down which we had come. . . . [H]e put some small stones on each side of the river to represent mountains. He then put down his hands, one on each side of the crooked mark and then raised them up again saying "e-e-e-e-e-e" as he raised them, to say that the mountains there were very high. Then he traced down the stream to a place below where we made our canoes; then he placed the stone back from the river farther, to show that there was a valley there, then he drew them in close again farther down, and piled them up again two or three tiers high, then placing both fists on them he raised them higher than the top of his head, saying "e-e-e-e-e-e" and looking still higher and shaking his head as if to say, "Awful bad canyon," and thus he went on describing the river till we understood him all right. It was all correct, which assured me that he knew all about the country.[15]

Wakara went on to tell Manly in graphic detail just what would happen to him and his men if they continued on down the river. The canoes would capsize, the Indian said, and all of them would drown. If that wasn't bad enough, he took his bow, and placing the point of an arrow at Manly's neck, demonstrated to him how the other Indians downstream would kill them. "He would draw his hand across his throat," Manly concluded, "and shut his eyes as if in death to make us understand that this was a hostile country before us, as well as rough and dangerous."

Armed with this explicit warning, Manly had a meeting with the rest of his men. He told them that "he would as soon be killed by Mormons as savage indians," and that their only hope was to strike out overland for Salt Lake City. All but two of the men agreed with their leader. These two, McMahon and Field, objected that the Indians could not be trusted; they must be planning an ambush. They would continue down the river, despite Wakara's warning.

The decision made, the forty-niners settled down to socializing with their new-found friends. Manly got into a target-shooting match with some of the young braves, "taking good care to beat them." They were impressed with his marksmanship and wanted to trade rifles with him, but he declined. A little later, Wakara approached Manly and invited him to go on the buffalo hunt. They were all in fine spirits, Wakara said, and would surely have a good hunt. Manly was tempted; the chief had indicated that the band would eventually get to Salt Lake City in the fall. Regretfully, however, Manly had to decline. The other men depended on him for food, and he would have to stay with them. It was not without second thoughts, though: "Had I been alone I think I should have accepted his offer, and should have had a good time."

Manly did a little horse-trading with Indians and got enough mounts to get himself and his remaining men over the mountains to the Mormon towns. Later that night, after all the trading and dickering had been concluded, they all relaxed and things got downright festive:

> When our plans were settled we felt in pretty good spirits again, and one of the boys got up a sort of corn-stalk fiddle which made a squeaking noise and in a little while there was a sort of mixed American and Indian dance going on in which the squaws joined and we had a pretty jolly time till quite late at night. We were well pleased that these wild folks had proved themselves to be true friends to us.[16]

That night, Manly had a dream in which he saw that going to Salt Lake was indeed the correct thing to do. This still wasn't enough for McMahon and Field, who didn't trust the Ute chief. The following morning, Manly and the rest of the boys parted company from the two dissenters:

> We shook hands with quivering lips as we each hoped the other would meet good luck, and find enough to eat and all such sort of friendly talk, and then with my little party on the one side and McMahon and Field, whom we were to leave behind, on the other, we bowed to each other with bared heads.[17]

After this farewell, Manly and his men mounted their Indian ponies and set off on the trail that Wakara had described to them. As he rode along, Manly reflected on the "wild folks" they had just met:

> The Indians here have the reputation of being bloodthirsty savages who took delight in murder and torture, but here in the very midst of this wild and desolate country we found a chief and his tribe, Walker and his followers, who were as humane and kind to white people as could be expected of any one. . . . He undoubtedly saved our little band from a watery grave, for without his advice we [would have] gone on and on, far into the great Colorado canyon, from which escape would have been impossible, while destruction by hostile Indians was among the strong probabilities of the case. So in a threefold way I have. . . . credited the lives of myself and my comrades to the thoughtful interest and humane consideration of old Chief Walker.[18]

Considering that in the pueblos and ranchos of California, Walker was feared second only to the devil himself, Manly's is an interesting assessment.

Wakara's instructions, like his map, proved to be completely accurate, although for the whites, unused to Indian ponies, it took exactly twice as long to get to Salt Lake City as the Ute chief had indicated. Far from being safe among the civilized settlements, however, Manly was just beginning his adventures. At Hobble Creek, in Utah Valley, he ran into Mr. Bennett, whom he was supposed to have accompanied across the plains in the first place. Mr. Bennett had decided to join a train heading for California by the Old Spanish Trail, which went to the south of the Sierras to Los Angeles. Manly went along, and when Mr. Bennett decided to follow a man who knew of a shortcut, Manly did too. It was not without some misgivings, however, in light of Manly's recent experience with shortcuts. The party had made a terrible mistake. The shortcut was actually the shortest path into the heart of Death Valley, which no white man had yet traveled through. It hadn't even been named until Manly's party blundered into it and some of them paid with their lives. Manly, rising to the occasion just as he had on the Green, took his river running companion John Rodgers and went for help. This time their ordeal was not from too much water, but from lack of it. Despite terrible thirst, they reached a rancho and were able to find help to come back and rescue the survivors.

Meanwhile, what of McMahon and Field? They followed the river into Desolation Canyon, but just as Wakara predicted, they were soon forced to abandon it. They tried to follow their comrades, but ran into the Ute chief, who took them along on his buffalo hunt. After leaving him in the fall, they faced further tribulations and had to eat old wolf skins to survive before they finally reached Salt Lake City.[19]

We know from Manly's account that there were other forty-niners who tried the river route to California before him. There were probably later parties of gold seekers, tempted by the smooth flow of the river at the emigrant crossing, who tried what seemed an easier route to the promised land. Of these there is no record, which makes Manly's all the more important. Equally fascinating as his experiences on the river are his descriptions of Wakara and the Utes at the height of their power in eastern Utah. Manly met the chief before he was disillusioned by the whites and tried unsuccessfully to rid his lands of them. For both of these accounts, the young Vermont adventurer deserves recognition.

A scant two decades later, America had changed, and those changes were filtering down to the Green River country. The gold rush to California was over, and the country had been through a bloody civil conflict that had only recently ended. Steel rails had replaced the rutted tracks of the ox trains. The days of the fur trappers, the free-roaming Indians, the buffalo, and the emigrant trains were almost over. Systematic scientific exploration and mapping of the West, interrupted by the Civil War, had been resumed with Clarence King's *Survey of the Fortieth Parallel.* It was time, in some men's minds, to begin to fill in those other blank places on the map that had so mystified and intrigued mapmakers and explorers.

4

Powell Surveys the River

Of all the parties that have floated the canyons of the upper Green since Ashley and his trappers in their bullboats, none is better known or better documented than the two expeditions led by John Wesley Powell.[1] In 1869 and 1871 he led a total of twenty-one men down the river; of these, no fewer than fifteen kept journals and diaries or wrote detailed letters that were published in newspapers all over the country. Major Powell himself wrote his own version of the trips, variously titled *The Exploration of the Colorado and Its Canyons*, or *Canyons of the Colorado*. Frederick S. Dellenbaugh, a member of the 1871 crew, in 1908 published his version of the journey, *A Canyon Voyage*, and retold the story of the 1869 trip in his earlier book, *The Romance of the Colorado*. For all this wealth of literature written about the expeditions, however, there have been no other explorations of the Green about which so much controversy or so many misconceptions exist. One common misconception is that Powell's account of the voyage is the only one that exists. The journals and letters of the other members on both expeditions, however, were gathered and published in various issues of the *Utah Historical Quarterly*. Another misconception is that both of Powell's expeditions were sponsored by the U.S. government. This was true of the 1871 journey, but the pioneering trip in 1869 was sponsored and partially funded by the Illinois Natural History Society. Powell and others of the crew paid some of the expenses out of their own pockets.[2] The only government support that the first expedition received was an order from Ulysses S. Grant authorizing the river explorers to draw their bacon and beans from U.S. Army posts.[3]

The most widely held and most erroneous view concerns the accuracy of Powell's book. Many regard it as gospel, and indeed one expects a scientific government report to be an accurate recounting of events and discoveries. This, unfortunately, is not the case. For reasons that are still not completely clear, Powell combined the events of both the 1869 and the 1871 journeys into one narrative, completely ignoring the crew and accomplishments of the second and attributing them to the first. He also switched times and places of certain events, consistently exaggerated the fall of the river to make the rapids appear more awesome than they were, and in a couple of cases actually made up events that are not corroborated by the other accounts.[4] Whatever the reasons, the fact remains that his report, however entertaining it might be to read, cannot be accepted as a historical document, but must be viewed as a Victorian travel romance.[5]

The story of these two epic voyages has almost always been told exclusively from Powell's viewpoint, or from sources particularly sympathetic to him, such as Dellenbaugh's books or William Culp Darrah's biography. The other members of both crews, however, left very vivid and interesting accounts of the journeys.

There are some crucial differences in the composition of the two crews that are vividly reflected in their journals and letters. The first crew consisted of Major Powell, his brother Walter H. Powell, George Young Bradley, John Colton Sumner, Oramel G. Howland, Seneca Howland, Bill Dunn, Billy Rhodes Hawkins, Frank Goodman, and Andy Hall. Billy Hawkins also went by W. H. Rhodes—he was said to be on the run from the law in Missouri, and tended to get nervous whenever he was around a sheriff. Almost all of these men were veterans of the Civil War, seasoned frontiersmen, or both. Their writings reveal an earthy, irreverent point of view. They were an independent lot, and viewed with a typical enlisted man's suspicion officers such as the Major and his brother, who had been a captain in the Union army. Members of the 1871 crew, by contrast, were almost all college educated, and were still living in the Midwest and East when the Major recruited them. Most of them were war veterans as well, but the similarities ended there.

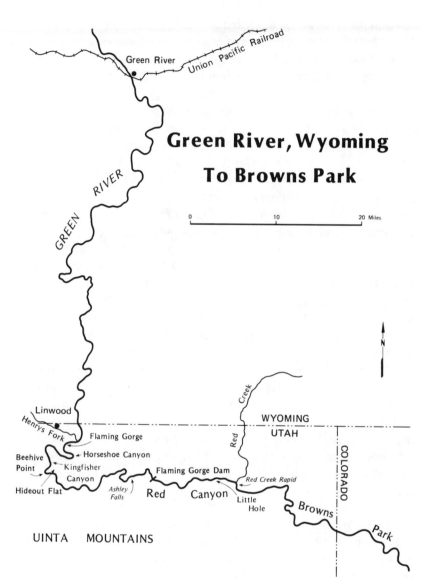

Green River, Wyoming
To Browns Park

Sumner, Hawkins, Dunn, and the Howland brothers had been with Major Powell since his initial explorations in Colorado the year before. While Powell may have had his sights set on the sweetness of scientific discovery, and a large appropriation from Congress if this survey was a success, these men had more immediate and palpable rewards in mind. They were planning to trap and prospect along the river. Sergeant George Bradley, who since 1867 had languished at the isolated Fort Steele in Wyoming Territory, had his own reasons for wanting to go along. He found service in the frontier army less exciting than the action he had seen during the Civil War, and was desperate to get out. As he himself put it, he "would be willing to explore the River Styx" for a discharge.[6] Powell arranged with the War Department for Bradley's release on the condition that he be a crew member on the expedition.

The backgrounds of the other men were equally varied. Some of them Powell recruited on the spot. Andy Hall was one of these, as was Frank Goodman, who showed up in Green River and begged to be taken along, apparently just for the adventure. Walter H. Powell had been a prisoner in the infamous Confederate prison at Camp Sorghum. The experience had affected his mind, and the Major hoped that the river journey would help him solve his mental problems.

The Major himself was well suited for both the hardship of the journey and the command. In his youth he had explored the Mississippi River and its tributaries in a small boat, and was thus well acquainted with river travel. His father had wished him to study for the ministry, but Powell preferred science, and so taught himself the rudiments of a number of subjects, such as natural history, philosophy, botany, and mathematics. He taught school and studied at a number of small colleges in the Midwest without receiving a degree from any of them. When the Civil War broke out in April 1860, he immediately joined the Union army as a private. By early summer he was a second lieutenant, by fall a captain. While commanding the artillery that was trying to stem the Confederate charge at the Battle of Shiloh in April 1862, his right arm was shattered by a minie ball just above the elbow, and amputated a few days later. Powell did not allow himself to be mustered out of the service, however, and after recovering from his wound he rejoined Grant's artillery command, and later participated in Sherman's march to the sea. After rising to the rank of major and command of the 17th Artillery Corps, Powell resigned his commission in January 1865. He was known as "Major" for the rest of his life.[7]

By the time the members of his crew began to gather at Green River in May 1869, Powell had already led three expeditions into Colorado and the Rocky Mountains in search of specimens and scientific knowledge under the auspices of the Illinois Natural History Society. On the last, in 1868, he had been seized by the idea of exploring the canyons of the Green and Colorado rivers.[8] When that year's expedition ended in the fall of 1868, Powell arranged for the men he had recruited to meet him at Green River the next May, while he went back east to see to the logistics and funding.

While Powell was arranging the details of the trip, Sumner, one of the Howland brothers, and Bill Dunn were making their way from the previous year's camp on the White River to the arranged rendezvous. Sumner wrote that they took their time, going by way of Browns Park and Fort Bridger, feasting on "duck soup and roasted ribs," having "lots of fun." Once they got to Green River, there were other diversions, as Sumner describes:

> We camped and awaited orders and in the meantime tried to drink all the whiskey there was in town. The result was a failure, as Jake Fields persisted in making it faster than we could drink it.[9]

On 12 May, the Major arrived from Chicago, where he had been among other things, supervising the construction of four boats that he had ordered for the expedition. They were to be shipped to the launch point on the newly completed railroad. Drawing on his experience on the deep, broad rivers of the Mississippi Valley, Powell had designed the boats accordingly. There were four, all with rounded bottoms, a deep draft, and space for two oarsmen and a steersman. Three were large freight boats, twenty-one feet long, built of oak, and double-ribbed for strength, with covered compartments fore and aft for buoyancy and storage. The other boat was built of pine and was only sixteen feet long. In the smaller boat, Powell would go first in line, inspecting the river and the rapids, signaling with flags to the other boats whether to continue or go ashore.[10]

Each of the three large boats carried about a ton of supplies, the usual army fare of the time: flour, sugar, beans, dried apples, salt pork, bacon, rice, coffee, tea. Since they were going into uncharted and uninhabited territory, they carried tools for repairing their craft, such as axes, augurs, and saws. Finally, since this was a scientific expedition, they carried instruments for making observations and measurements, such as barometers, sextants, and chronometers. Supplies, tools, and instruments were to be divided equally among the three large boats so that the loss of one would not cripple the expedition. The method Powell planned to use for getting through rapids was for the two oarsmen to face upstream, rowing with all their might, while the man in the stern sat at the steering oar and provided direction. The great speed, it was thought, would give the steersman control over the boat.

Besides the boats, Powell also brought from Chicago a prospective crew member, a "young scientific duck," as Sumner called him. His college education and youth did not endear him to the "old soldiers" of the crew:

> [He] was not at all necessary. However, he did not give us much time to imbibe his wisdom, as he stayed only one day. One good look at the Green River and the gang was enough. He vamoosed the camp that night, and we were left in darkness, mourning bitterly.[11]

The young scholar, unused to the rough-and-tumble ways of the frontier, did not seem to like camp life and especially camp cooking. One day, when Captain Powell wanted to wash his socks, Hawkins, who was cook for the crew, gave him a small camp kettle, which he set by the fire. The day's coffee was in a large kettle that hid the smaller one from sight. Everyone except the newcomer was complimenting Hawkins on the coffee, when Sumner decided to play a joke on the young scientist:

> Sumner said there was something mighty peculiar about the coffee, and asked me what was the matter with it. I took my bowie knife and stuck it in one of the Captain's socks and held it up over the kettle just back of the coffee. With the reddish water running off, it looked just as though I had taken it out of the coffee kettle. I yelled "Who in hell put his socks in the coffee?" All said they had not except the young man, who did not answer. When I asked him if he had, he said very politely that he had not, but he was getting up and leaving at the time. That was the last we ever saw of him.[12]

Finally, on 24 May, all preparations were complete, and the expedition set off from Green River in high spirits, "after much blowing off of gas and the fumes of bad whiskey."[13] The boats had all been christened: the *Emma Dean*, the light boat, named after the Major's wife and crewed by Powell, Bill Dunn, and Sumner; the *Maid of the Canyon*, with Walter Powell and George Bradley; *Kitty Clyde's Sister*, "manned by as jolly a brace of boys as ever swung a whip over a lazy ox," Billy Hawkins, and Andy Hall; and the *No Name,* a "piratic craft," manned by O. G. Howland, his brother Seneca, and Frank Goodman.[14]

Unaccustomed to their new mode of travel, some of the men had difficulty adjusting at first:

> As *Kitty's* crew [has] been using the whip more of late years than the oars, she ran on a sand-bar in the middle of the river, got off of that, and ran ashore on the east side, near the mouth of Bitter Creek, but finally got off and came down to the rest of the fleet in gallant style, her crew swearing she would not "gee" or "haw" a "cuss."[15]

Spirits were still high when they made their first camp. Bradley and Dunn went hunting, and returned with a small rabbit. After dinner, Sumner wrote, they sat around the campfire and "exchanged tough stories at a fearful rate," a practice still followed by river runners. Camp was early, though; the protracted good-byes from the populace of Green River had taken their toll: "We turned in early, as most of the men had been up for several preceding nights, taking leave of their many friends, 'a la Muscovite.' The natural consequences were fog[g]y ideas and snarly hair."[16]

Despite the frequent groundings and their unfamiliarity with the new boats, they made good time on the swift, smooth river. On 27 May, they approached the first of the many canyons they would traverse in the next few months—Flaming Gorge:[17]

> [W]e entered the mouth of the first canyon and encamped amid the cottonwood trees surrounded by bluffs 1220 ft. high and on one side nearly perpendicular. It is the grandest scenery I have found in the mountains and I am delighted with it. I went out to see the country this morning and found it grand beyond conception. The river winds like a serpent through between nearly perpendicular cliffs 1200 ft. high but instead of rapids it is deep and calm as a lake.[18]

They passed through the next two canyons, Horseshoe and Kingfisher, without trouble, marveling at the scenery and trying in vain to add the elusive mountain sheep to their larder. On the last day of the month, they entered Red Canyon and encountered their first real rapid. Now began the labor of portaging and lining; as they went deeper and deeper into the canyons, the men must have often cursed the Major's choice of oak for the boats, no matter how sturdy. They had to get used to it, however, for they would be either lining or portaging for the next three months.

The next day they came to Ashley Falls, which took them all day to pass. The men named this rapid after the earlier explorer whose name Powell saw on the cliff above the rapid. Apparently no one had noticed Manly's similar inscription just upstream. Red Canyon was not all rocks and rapids, however. On 2 June, Sumner described the rest of their voyage through Red Canyon:

> [O]ff we go down the river; beautiful river, that increases its speed . . . till a perfect rapid all the way, but clear of sunken rocks; so we run through the waves at express speed; made seventeen miles through Red Stone Canyon in less than an hour running time, the boats bounding through the waves like a school of porpoise. The *Emma* being very light is tossed about in a way that threatens to shake her to pieces, and is nearly as hard to ride as a Mexican pony. We plunge along singing, yelling, like drunken sailors, all feeling that such rides do not come every day. It was like sparking a black-eyed girl—just dangerous enough to be exciting.[19]

Since almost all of the men had seen service in the Civil War (Andy Hall was the only exception), they were bound to indulge at one time or another in that time-honored tradition and privilege of enlisted men: griping. The Major and his brother, being former officers, were of course above this sort of thing, but not so the rest of the crew. The most persistent and biting was Bradley. His dry and sarcastic wit was most often directed at the hunters for the party, although, as he demonstrated later, even the Major himself was not safe from his barbs. He comments on the prowess of the hunters:

> June 2, 1869—The men are out hunting and have not yet come in but if they have their usual luck we shall have bacon for breakfast.
> June 3, 1869—The last hunter is in and if we were dependent on them for subsistence we should be as fat as "Job's turkey" in a few weeks, for they didn't bring in enough game for a grease spot.[20]

This was just a warm-up, however. On 14 June he wound up and really let fly:

> The men have all come in from hunting, as ever without game. We frequently see mountain sheep as we pass along, and if we kept *still* we might kill them but as soon as we land the men begin to shoot and make a great noise and the game for miles around is allarmed and takes back from the river. This makes one think that these are not *hunters* and I believe that if left to maintain themselves with their rifles they would fare worse than Job's turkey. They seem more like school-boys on a holiday than like men accustomed to live by the chase, but as I am no hunter myself I must not criticize others. Still as usual I have my opinion.[21]

On 3 June, Sumner had some acid comments about the fish they caught in the river:

> [S]ome of the boys got out the fishing tackle and soon had the bank covered with a queer mongrel of mackerel, sucker and whitefish; the other an afflicted cross of white fish and lake trout. Take a piece of raw pork and a paper of pins, and make a sandwich, and you have the mongrels. Take out the pork and you have a fair sample of the edible qualities of the other kinds. [22]

That same day found the explorers back in familiar territory— Browns Park. As the men learned, however, they were not the only party to float the Green River that May. On 4 June, Bradley mentions seeing a boat belonging to two men, apparently prospectors, who had preceded Powell and his crew by a few days into the canyons. Although Bradley didn't see them, he did see their tracks, so they must have made the voyage safely. Another party, however, that left a few days after Powell's was not so lucky. This group of fifteen miners led by a Mr. Hook of Cheyenne, whose first name is variously reported as "H. M." or "Theodore," left Green River on 1 June. Hook declared that if any one-armed pilgrim from back east could make it through the canyons, why then he could too. Their crude boats proved unequal to the canyon, though, and Hook paid for the boast with his life. The others, quite the worse for wear, left the river and made their way back to Green River. [23] In writing about the accident two years later, Frederick Dellenbaugh, a crew member on the 1871 expedition, could not refrain from a note of condescension:

> One rapid where Theodore Hook, of Cheyenne, was drowned in 1869, while attempting to follow the first party, gave us no trouble. We sailed through it easily. Hook had declared that if Powell could descend the river he could too, and headed a party to follow. The motive I believe was prospecting. I do not know how far they expected to go but this was as far as they got. Their abandoned boats, flat-bottomed and inadequate, still lay half-buried in sand on the left-hand bank, and not far off on a sandy knoll was the grave of the unfortunate leader marked by a pine board set up, with his name painted on it. Old sacks, ropes, oars, etc., emphasized the completeness of the disaster. [24]

Back in Browns Park, the men rested from their labors in the canyons above during the five days they spent floating through the valley. There was time for fishing, writing letters or catching up on journals, mending clothes or just plain loafing. They tried hunting, but as Bradley noted, didn't have much success. All of them were impressed by the potential of Browns Park for raising cattle, and Sumner wrote that the winter before he had seen four thousand head of oxen pastured there.[25]

The scientific work of the expedition had to go on at the same time. Every day, the Major took readings with the barometer to determine altitude, and with the sextant to find their position. On the fifth, Bradley and two others went across the river to survey the bluffs. O. G. Howland, who was a printer and in charge of the topographical work for the expedition, spent the time completing his map of the canyons already traversed. Powell climbed Douglas Mountain, on the south side of the valley, to take a barometer reading. The men made other observations as well:

> This morning we were all awakened by the wild birds singing in the old tree above our heads. The sweet songs of birds, the fragrant odor of wild roses, the low, sweet rippling of the ever murmuring river at sunrise in the wilderness, made everything as lovely as a poets dream. I was just wandering into paradise; could see the dim shadow of the dark-eyed houris, when I was startled by the cry, "Roll out; bulls in the corral; chain up the gaps"— our usual call to breakfast. The hour is vanished, and I rolled out to fried fish and hot coffee.[26]

It was just as well that they had those few idyllic days of still water and bird song, for their camp on 7 June was at the end of Browns Park. Despite the rustling of cottonwood leaves, the warm days, and the dreams of "dark-eyed houris," the men must have often glanced to where the river entered the mountains just downstream, which has been described as "a mountain drinking a river" by one of the early settlers of the park. Powell had been to Browns Park on horseback in 1868, and had climbed up on the rim of Lodore and looked over, so he knew how deep and dark the canyon was. Back at Green River, the old-timers had no doubt told them plenty of stories about those foolish enough to try to navigate the canyons. With these happy thoughts in mind, they must have often felt a thrill of apprehension as they approached the end of Browns Park, watching the "black portal into a region of gloom"—the Gates of Lodore—draw ever nearer.

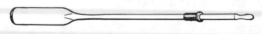

8 June 1869. The expedition got an early start that morning. A good thing, too, as their troubles began almost as soon as they entered the canyon. They navigated a number of small but fierce rapids without

Gates of Lodore.

difficulty, even though they had to line their boats in a couple of places. Soon, however, they came to the worst rapid they had yet seen and ran into serious trouble. The Major, seeing that the rapid could not be run safely, signaled the other three boats to pull for shore, but the *No Name,* with the Howland brothers and Frank Goodman, somehow missed the signal. O. G. Howland described what happened next:

> About one o'clock the signal boat signaled at the foot of a very bad rapid to go ashore; boats nearly full of water—two were made fast, but owing to not understanding the signal, the crew of the ''No Name'' failed very effectually, owing in the main, to having so much water aboard as to make her nearly or quite unmanageable; otherwise, the mistake was seen by us in time to save her. Our next move after failing to get in, was to run her as long as she would float, and gradually work her ashore on a bar below, where from the spray and foam, showed shoal water. She sunk, however, striking rocks as she passed along, until she was stove up so bad that there was no use to stay by her any longer, so the crew all at the same time concluded quickly to strike for the bar.

All three men had been knocked from the boat, but managed to cling to her until they reached the bar. The Howlands got there first and were able to snatch Goodman from a large boulder. During all of this,

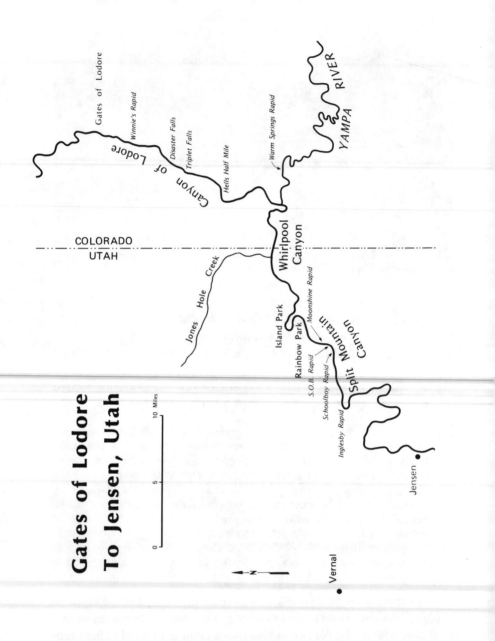

Gates of Lodore
To Jensen, Utah

those on shore were rushing down to our help, but we so completely out-
distanced them in our ride through the waves, that we were out of sight
wholly before we struck the bar. We did not any of us receive any serious
injury, barely a few bumps on our shins as the waves dashed us against
the rocks in the shoal. Our sand bar had a large pine trunk drifted upon
it, from the pitch of which, after drying our matches, we succeeded in
starting a fire. Our position on the sand bar began to look serious, as the
water was rapidly rising, so much so, that what were boulders imbedded
in the sand when we landed, was getting like the shoal above. However,
Mr. Sumner, as soon as they could let the little boat down to us and dump
her cargo, crossed the channel to where we could reach his boat. We then
turned the boat up among the shoals as far as we could stand, and wade,
when three got in her and the other held her nose until they got their oars
in position ready for a sharp venture. Her nose was pushed into the current, the oars playing rapidly, struck one rock, tilting us up at an angle
of forty-five degrees, off in the foam below and struck shore twenty-five
yards above a perfect hell of foam, safe and sound, barring a few bruises
and a slight ducking.[27]

"We were as glad to shake hands with them," Powell wrote, "as though
they had been on a voyage around the world, and wrecked on a distant
coast."[28]

In this disaster they lost two thousand pounds of provisions and the
entire outfits of the three crewmen, including extra clothes, bedding,
guns, knives, and belts plus all the topographic notes and the map that
the elder Howland had made. A more serious loss, at least to the Major, was all of the barometers, which had been inadvertently stowed
on the ill-fated boat. He spent an anxious night pacing the sand wondering how the scientific purposes of the trip could be carried out without them. At one point he considered climbing out of the canyon and
going to Salt Lake City to try and obtain replacements.

The next morning, however, they could see that the aft compartment of the boat was still lodged among the rocks, and after some deliberation, Powell decided to try and recover whatever was in it. Sumner
and Dunn volunteered to take the small boat over and make the attempt.
To Powell's great joy, the barometers were in the cabin, and to the
delight of the men, there was a "blue keg"—a three-gallon jug of
whiskey—which had also survived intact.

According to Robert Brewster Stanton, who surveyed the Colorado
twenty years after Powell and later compiled a mammoth history of the
river, the loss of the *No Name* was the beginning of trouble between
the Major and the elder Howland. Powell criticized Howland for not

responding to the signal in time; Howland countered that the signal was late, and improperly given. There was doubt that the signal was given at all. Given the speed with which things happen in rapids, even a properly given signal might not have been in time. At any rate, tensions between the two men increased, in part because of the inadequate food supply caused by the loss of the *No Name*'s cargo. It could have contributed to the break-up of the party at the bottom of the Grand Canyon. What really caused the split is impossible to say at this late date, but there is little doubt that the men felt the loss of the provisions and tools for the remainder of the voyage.[29]

It took them four days of hard labor to complete the portage around the rest of the rapid, working all the while "like galley slaves." Bradley still found time to criticize the Major's choice of camping places, however: "The Major as usual has chosen the worst camping-ground possible. If I had a dog that would lie where my bed is made tonight, I would kill him and burn his collar and swear I never owned him."[30]

They named this rapid, appropriately, Disaster Falls. It was only the first of a series of difficult rapids they would have to pass. For the next ten days they lined or portaged their heavy, awkward boats past more rapids, lugged their sacks of flour and sides of bacon over trails they had to build themselves, or slipped and fell amongst the moss-covered boulders by the side of the river. The roar of the rapids was unceasing; the rocks beneath their feet shook with the thunder of the crashing waters. No one really says so, but the oppressive gloom of the canyon must have begun to take its toll on them, just as it had on Ashley's trappers a half-century before. At Triplet Falls, Harp Falls, Hell's Half Mile, and a host of smaller rapids, the men had to unload, line, reload. Otis Marston, a famous river-historian and no admirer of Powell's, said of this portion of Powell's journey: "A significant part of the mileage had been overland, and one of the basic scientific facts established had been that most of the rapids had shores adequate for lining and portaging."[31]

Rapids and wrecks were not the only dangers they had to contend with, however. On 16 June, they were camped at Alcove Brook, a lovely spot near the mouth of Lodore, when a gust of wind scattered their camp-fire into the underbrush. The fire spread so quickly that the men barely had time to save themselves. They jumped into the boats, and had to immediately run a small rapid just downstream. Most of them were singed or suffered minor burns, and many of the men lost personal items that had to be left behind in the rush. A more serious loss was almost all of their cooking utensils and pots, for which, Howland ruefully noted, "we felt the need quite often."

Their problems still weren't over for the day, for later one of the boats got away from them while they were lining it. Hawkins and Sumner had a harrowing ride down a rapid before they caught up with it, just at the head of the next rapid. Finally, on 18 June they passed the Mitten Park Fault and drifted down to the mouth of the Yampa. Bradley spoke for all of them when he recorded a relieved and optimistic note that day:

> I predict that the river will improve from this point, for the more water there is the wider channel it will make for itself and the less liability will there be of its falling in and blocking up clear across, and if there is one side clear we can run it or at least have one good side to let down the boats with ropes.[32]

Here at last was a respite from the crashing waters and the gloom of the bottom of Lodore. Echo Park in June is an enchanting place, the air full of bird song and the sweet smell of new grass. The days are warm without the choking heat of August, and the mosquitoes are present, but not in full force. At night the gentle murmur of the river and the breeze in the cottonwood leaves lulls the weary traveler to sleep. Powell's crew took full advantage of the three-day layover. There was time to repair the boats, battered and leaky after the hard ten days above. Some of them fished, while others did their mending—the long johns that were standard apparel for running rapids had had a hard time of it as well. Some of them amused themselves listening to the marvelous echoes that rebounded from the cliffs opposite the campsite, which inspired the name Echo Park. On Hall's suggestion, they named the canyon they had just run Lodore Canyon, after a poem he remembered from a childhood reader. Even though the name came from a poem about a waterfall on a stream near Derwentwater in the Lake District of northwest England, it seems strangely appropriate. As one modern writer put it:

> Lodore: a word full of dolorous long O sounds, a heavily romantic name that matches a sonorous canyon. . . . Despite objections from a chauvinistic member of the crew who felt that it was wrong to apply a foreign-inspired title to an American canyon, it became Lodore and it could be nothing else.[33]

The "chauvinistic" crew member was Sumner, who said of the Major's choice of name for the canyon "the idea of diving into musty trash to find names for new discoveries on a new continent is un-American, to say the least!"[34]

Much refreshed by their rest, the men resumed their journey on 21 June, drifting around the corner from Echo Park and into Whirlpool Canyon. Whirlpool can be almost as dark and threatening as Lodore, but the channel is generally free of rocks, producing a thrilling roller-coaster ride. They were able to make good time, running all the way down to Jones Hole with only two portages. A few minutes in the latter place produced a fine batch of trout for supper that night. The next day a short, smooth run brought them to the end of the canyon. Sumner describes the day's run:

> Dancing over the waves that had never before been disturbed by any keel, the walls getting gradually lower, till about four o'clock, when we came suddenly out into a splendid park; the river widened out into a stream as large as the Missouri, with a number of islands in it covered with cottonwood trees.[35]

Bradley, though, expressed a sense of relief common to most travelers on the Green:

> [A]fter a run of about 5 miles more we came out into an exceedingly beautiful valley full of islands covered with grass and cottonwood. After passing so many days in the dark canyons where there is little but bare rocks we feel very much pleased when for a few days we enjoy the valley.[36]

In late June, when Powell's crew passed through Island Park, it is just beginning to become oppressively hot out in the sagebrush flats. Under the cottonwoods, though, it is still cool and shady, a perfect place to rest from the strenuous passage of the canyons above and to prepare for the last canyon, Split Mountain.

Split Mountain has the sharpest drop of all the upper canyons of the Green, with four major rapids and many smaller ones. The men were looking forward to putting it behind them, for while climbing the mountains around Island Park, they had seen that after this last canyon, the river ran through quiet water as far as they could see. Even though they were getting quite skilled at portaging and lining, and at running rapids when they got the opportunity, they were ready for some quiet water.

Split Mountain with the Uinta Basin in the distance.

First, though, there was the canyon. Howland described their passage:

> On the 25th we again started on our way, running down four miles and turning off in a tangent; towards the east we entered the canyon. Soon began to appear rapids which followed one upon the other, in rapid succession. Today we made two portages and camped at the head of another rapid, where we shall have to make another portage tomorrow. . . .
>
> June 26th—We made our portage of provisions, let down our boats and pulled them out upon the rocks on the beach, last night. If we had not done so the waves would have rolled them about upon the rocks so much as to have worn them badly. This morning we landed our boats, loaded up, ran down six miles to the head of the falls and made portage of a hundred yards. From here we ran with a good many short twists and whirls out into the valley.[37]

On that same day, near the end of the canyon, they stopped so the Major could do some fossil hunting. With this dim view of the proceedings, Sumner proved that Bradley didn't have a monopoly on griping. "While the men were at work, the Professor [Powell] climbed up the sidehills looking for fossils; spent two hours to find one, and came back to find a peck that the men had picked up on the bank of the river."[38]

He was as glad as everyone else, though, when they reached the end of Split Mountain canyon. "[A]ll at once the great Uinta Valley spread out before us as far as the eye could reach. It was a welcome sight to us after two weeks of the hardest kind of work, in a canyon where we could not see half a mile, very often, in any direction but straight up. All hands pulled with a will. . . ."[39]

By the twenty-eighth, they were camped at the mouth of the Uinta River, their interim destination. Here they would rest while the Major went upriver to the Ute Indian agency, about twenty miles away, for supplies, mail, and news. He left on 2 July, with Hawkins and Goodman. Meanwhile, the rest of the crew fished, hunted the wildfowl in the marshes nearby, and most of all slapped mosquitoes. The little pests were especially bad along the river, as Bradley recorded on the day the Major left:

> One of the men says that while out on the shore of the lake [Pelican Lake] a mosquito asked him for his pipe, knife and tobacco and told him to hunt his old clothes for a match while he loaded the pipe—but I didn't hear the mosquito ask him though there are some very large ones here.[40]

The men were, all in all, pretty pleased with themselves. The old-timers back in Green River had told them they would never get as far as Browns Park, let alone all the way to the Uinta Basin. True, they had lost a boat, but that could have happened to anyone—at least they hadn't lost any of the crew.

Or had they? The Major returned the next day from the agency with more provisions, newspapers, and mail, but without Frank Goodman. For his decision to leave at this point, Goodman has always gotten a bad deal from chroniclers of the Powell journeys, usually being derisively referred to as "the florid-faced Englishman." Dellenbaugh calls him a deserter, and Darrah dismisses him with this short statement: "Goodman had no particular skill or training which would have suited him for the work. . . . [H]e proved to be rather useless."[41]

Frank Goodman, however, should not be dismissed so quickly. When Powell was organizing his expedition at Green River, the departure of the "young scientific duck" left the party a man short, and Goodman asked to be included in the crew. When the *No Name* was wrecked, he lost everything he owned except for the pair of shoes and the red long-handled underwear he was wearing. Later historians who have such a low opinion of Frank Goodman have tended to ignore this fact, but the loss of his entire outfit must be taken into consideration. Had he continued, he would have been completely dependent on the rest of the crew for everything, even clothes. This could not have been a very pleasing prospect. At any rate, he stayed around the Uinta Basin for the rest of his life. Goodman moved a small band of sheep into Browns Park and prospered for a while, but was driven out by cattlemen in 1897. He moved to Vernal with his second wife, and lived there until he died in 1913. He is buried in the Vernal Cemetery. A grandson, Manuel Goodman, still lives in Dinosaur, Colorado, not far from where his grandfather briefly entered the pages of history.[42]

Powell and his crew resumed their journey on 6 July and were soon back in the canyons, lining, portaging, sweating, slapping mosquitos, griping. After an arduous journey, they reached the Grand Wash Cliffs, the end of the Grand Canyon, in late August. Two years later, in May of 1871, a small group of men in three boats were getting ready to push off into the flood-swollen river. Passengers on the Union Pacific, lethargic from the endless journey across the Wyoming plains, sat up and took notice. The citizens of Green River, though, and especially the "wise men" of Jake Field's store, were by now getting used to this sort of thing. They sagely wagged their heads—another bunch of damn-fool easterners getting ready to risk their necks where no man had a right to be. Would these pilgrims never learn?

The Second Colorado River
Exploring Expedition

Even before he ended his first expedition at the mouth of the Virgin River in August 1869, Major Powell knew he would have to make another trip. The first one had, at the end, turned into a race for survival. The men were living on dough gods—little more than cooked lumps of moldy flour—sour dried apples, and coffee. The rapids had, despite Bradley's optimistic prediction back at the end of Lodore, become worse and worse. Scientific observation and topographic mapping were shunted aside in the day-to-day struggle just to stay alive. Finally, they had come to one rapid that all agreed was the worst they had ever seen, and the party split up. The two groups of men went their separate ways, each convinced the other was making a serious mistake. In order to fulfill his true purpose—making an accurate and detailed survey of the course of the river—Powell knew another voyage would be necessary. He also felt he owed it to the three who left the party to find out what had become of them.[1]

The publicity that the first trip had generated in the nation's newspapers had caused a usually stingy Congress to shake loose a $10,000 appropriation to fund the Major's continued survey. They even made it official, giving it equal status with the surveys of the western lands

The start of John Wesley Powell's second expedition at Green River, Wyoming, 22 May 1871.

already in progress led by Clarence King and Ferdinand V. Hayden.[2] Powell's survey would be called the Geographical and Geological Survey of the Rocky Mountain Region.[3]

The second expedition was to be much better equipped than the first. The Major, learning something from the first trip, had three new boats built. These would be of the same design as the first—he still believed that the round bottom and deep draft were the best design for river running—but with the addition of a much-needed compartment amidships for cargo and buoyancy. On the first trip, only the Major had worn a life preserver, because with only one arm he could not swim well. On the second, all crew members were provided with inflatable rubber life belts.[4] Powell planned to carry a bulky wet-plate camera to make a photographic record of the canyons as they went along. The men hated it, for it was cumbersome weight to lug up the side of a mountain for a photograph or along the side of the river during a portage. Clem Powell, who was the assistant to the photographer and had to carry the camera, complained bitterly and often about it in his journal calling it the "infernal mountain howitzer." The invaluable photographic record of the canyons it provided, however, turned out to be worth the effort.

Ensuring an adequate food supply was another of Powell's priorities. He had made arrangements in advance with Pardon Dodds and Jacob Hamblin, both well-known frontiersmen and Indian scouts, to meet the river party with pack trains of extra provisions at designated places along the route. The near-starvation that had contributed to the premature end of the first expedition would not be a problem on this trip.[5]

The biggest difference between Powell's two expeditions, however, was in the composition of the crews. The Major was determined that there would be no whiskey drinking, grumbling, irreverent frontiersmen along, who would make sport of the young scientists favored by Powell, or who would be contemptuous of the Major's authority. Powell chose very carefully men he knew well and who he had worked with in the past. The second-in-command and chief topographer, for example, was Almon Harris Thompson, Powell's brother-in-law and a well-known geologist and topographer. For assistants to the "Prof," as Thompson was generally called, Powell chose Stephen V. Jones, John F. Steward, and Francis Marion Bishop. E. O. Beaman, an experienced photographer from New York, was chosen for that post, with Walter Clement Powell, the Major's young cousin, for his assistant. The youngest member of the expedition was seventeen-year-old Frederick S. Dellenbaugh, an art student from New York who left for the trip without telling his parents for fear they would withhold permission. For camp help, Powell chose Andy Hattan, with Frank Richardson as general assistant. Jack Hillers, a teamster from Salt Lake City, was hired to replace Jack Sumner, the only member of the first expedition to be invited to accompany the second. Sumner was on his way to join the crew in Green River when he was detained by late spring snows in Colorado and was unable to meet at the rendezvous. Hillers took his place, later became assistant to Beaman, and still later became a noted photographer in his own right.

Almost all of these men were college educated, sober, serious, scientifically minded, and, in the case of Bishop and Jones at least, quite religious. All of them knew how to do their assigned tasks, and furthermore, they could take orders. All of them except Clem Powell, Dellenbaugh, and Richardson had been soldiers in the Civil War. Steward and the Major had met in 1863 while they were looking for fossils in the trenches around Vicksburg, Mississippi, during the siege of that city. Later scholars have questioned why Powell, knowing the roughness of the water and the rapids, did not recruit for his second trip some men skilled in the handling of small craft such as French-Canadian voyageurs. As it turned out, the second expedition fared better in the rapids than the first, although they had their share of near-misses. Per-

Jake Fields's store, Green River, Wyoming, 1871.

haps Powell was more interested in having a crew that would obey his orders than one with rough-water experience, who might later prove to be rebellious.[6]

The "Second Colorado River Exploring Expedition" left Green River on 22 May 1871, almost two years to the day after the first. Just about the whole population of the town came to see them off, although as Dellenbaugh records, "None of the chinamen came down, and there were no Indians in town that day." As it was, the whole population "did not make a crowd." The "wise men" who lounged on the porch of Jake Fields's store warned them not to go. Hadn't they heard about Hook drowning less than two years ago? And everyone knew that some of the Major's men had not made it home from the first expedition. Were they unaware of the whirlpools and waterfalls and the dreaded Green River Suck? They would never make it to Browns Park, the wags predicted, let alone California.

Powell's men were confident in their boats and in the Major, however, and were undaunted by the doomsayers of Fields's Store. The new boats were gaily decked out in fresh white paint and snappy green canvas hatch covers. In addition, each sported an American flag made by Mrs. Thompson, with the name of the boat on one side and the stars and stripes on the other. How could anything go wrong?

The names of the boats and their crew were: the *Emma Dean*, again named for Powell's wife, manned by the Major, Jones, Hillers, and Dellenbaugh; the *Nellie Powell*, after Mrs. Thompson, with Thompson, Steward, Bishop, and Richardson; and the *Cañonita*, crewed by Beaman, Hattan, and Clem Powell.[7] The expedition departed in the afternoon and floated along gaily on the swollen river. Spirits were high; they were off on a grand scientific adventure in the spirit of Lewis and Clark, and they knew it. The tensions and personality conflicts that would enliven later journal entries were not yet in evidence. This crew had more success at hunting than the first as well. Three days out they flushed some deer while passing an island and shot three of them. Things were off to a good start. Their camp on 27 May was at the entrance to Flaming Gorge, and all of them were impressed with the beauty of the flaring red rocks.

In Horseshoe Canyon, they ran their first rapid. E. O. Beaman left the following breathless description of the experience, which was later published in *Appleton's Journal*:

> At this place we ran our first dangerous rapid. Immense bowlders cleft the rapid current, past which our boat shot at the rate of twenty miles an hour, missing destruction by what seemed a hair's-breadth, and finding beyond not smooth water, but waves, dashing wildly from six to eight feet high. Nor did we escape without a thorough drenching.[8]

On the second of June their "hard work and lively times" began. As Thompson recorded, the crew of the *Nellie Powell* missed the Major's signal, and ran into potential disaster:

> [W]e went into the rapids; ran three, when we came to a short turn in the river to right, then immediately to left with rocks in both bends. We were steering all right to take advantage of the current when the Major motioned us in farther to the right. He made motions so energetically that we thought we must come in, so putting forth all our strength I threw her bow up stream and made for the bank. I soon found that we were too far in, so tried all we could to bring her round. It was too late, we could not come in and drifted on the rocks just as she filled, caught the rope and held her. In about a minute we got the rope up stream, pulled the boat out from the bank when she righted and we pulled her up on the beach. [We] [p]artially unloaded, repaired the broken side, towed up to a good point for a start, took the very same course as we were taking at first, [and] ran the rapid without shipping a drop.[9]

What Thompson does not mention in his description is that Richardson was trapped under the boat, and might have drowned had Thompson not reached down and pulled him to safety. The damage to the *Nellie Powell* was not the only casualty; the *Emma Dean* also struck a rock and lost an oarlock.

Sobered by this demonstration of just how fast they could get into trouble, they took their time through the next few rapids, portaging the supplies and lining the boats, and running rapids only after careful inspection. Just downstream from their first portage, they ran the rapid where Hook had drowned two years previously. The abandoned boats, camp gear, oars and other equipment, in addition to the melancholy grave on the hillside above the rapid, emphasized the need for caution.

On the afternoon of 5 June they came to Ashley Falls. They carried one boat around, decided that that was too much work, and tried to line the next one through. The boat shot through the channel, almost pulling Dellenbaugh into the river, and banged sharply on the rocks. No doubt mindful of the long walk back to the railroad and the grave just upstream, they decided that they would not risk the other boat. Camp that night was at the foot of the falls, and as they sat around the fire, Steward remarked that the canyon was so impressive that it would be "worth a journey across the continent."

Below the falls, the Major told them, they would have no more rapids until they reached the Canyon of Lodore. The next morning, however, they had not gone far when they turned a corner and there was a small rapid. "Down the river we went," remarked Hillers, "meeting rappids after rappids. . . . [A]t dinner some one of the boys asked the Major if we would have any more smooth water, when he answered 'Well about the same'."[10]

After two more days in Red Canyon, they entered Browns Park. Here they met a party of Texans who had wintered a herd of 8,500 cattle there and who were preparing to move them on to Montana. The cattlemen, the Harrell brothers and another man named Bacon, had brought mail and news for Powell's crew, a pleasant surprise. All hands devoted the rest of the day to devouring the welcome letters from home.[11]

At this camp, Richardson decided to leave the expedition, or the Major decided for him. There was some indication earlier that he was not fitting into the group—Clem Powell noted that he left at Major Powell's request—but they were all sorry to see him go.[12] Arrangements were made with the cattlemen for Richardson to accompany them back to Green River, and the Texans further agreed to take specimens, letters, and telegrams with them, and to pick up more mail for the expedition and meet them a few days later at the Gates of Lodore.

With that happy prospect in mind, and with their larder considerably augmented by some fresh beef from the cattlemen, they resumed their river journey. The next week, while they drifted the forty miles to the end of Browns Park, was an idyllic one for the men. They floated along lazily, the boats lashed together, listening while the Major read aloud from *The Lady of the Lake*, admiring the scenery, or swimming alongside the boats. They stopped now and then to take observations and hunt for game. About this time, for reasons that he kept to himself, the Major changed the name to Browns Park.[13]

They reached the end of the park on 16 June and camped for a few days to take observations and measurements from the cliffs at the Gates of Lodore and to await the return of the Texans with the mail. June in Browns Park is the height of the mosquito hatch, and the men suffered greatly from those that infested the river bottoms.

On the seventeenth, a messenger arrived with the disappointing news that their mail had already been forwarded on to their next planned stop, the Ute Agency on the Uinta River, and, consequently, it would be a month or more before they could get their next news from home. There was nothing left to do but start down the Canyon of Lodore. All hands recorded an eagerness and a sense of relief at getting back into the boats. They were ready to meet the challenge and get away from the clouds of mosquitoes.

The river wastes no time in Lodore, and by the time they camped that night, at the head of a rocky little rapid, they had already run four others. The next morning everyone climbed up into the charming grotto just above their camp. "Ah, but tis a beautiful place," Clem commented, and Jones elaborated further:

> Just below camp . . . a beautiful grotto was found, extending back several hundred feet, the walls nearly meeting above, the interior hollowed out and opening at the rear by a succession of immense steps to the top of the cliff, while a tiny streamlet of the purest water trickled down through the rocks, whose moist sides were covered with pendulous moss, from which the water dripped in little streams. Huge masses of rock have fallen from the roof and sides in places nearly obstructing the passage.[14]

At Steward's request, they named the place Winnie's Grotto after his young daughter. (The rapid below, the first of any difficulty in Lodore, is now known as Winnie's Rapid.)

That same day brought them to the head of Disaster Falls, and if there were any lingering doubts about the power of the river, one look at the "foaming, raging mass of water" must have dispelled them. While landing, Beaman in the *Cañonita* made the same mistake that O. G. Howland had made two years before. The photographer waited too long and was almost carried over the falls. "All hands stood aghast for a moment," says Hillers. "Five feet more and he would have shared the fate of the *No Name*.[15] Reminders of the latter boat's sad fate were not lacking. Pieces of the wrecked craft were strewn about, and the men found two oars and a sack of flour left from the wreck. They kept the oars because they broke a lot of them maneuvering the heavy boats. The sack of flour, to their surprise, was in excellent condition. "Notwithstanding its exposure to the weather for more than two years, a hard crust had formed on the outside about half an inch thick, the flour thus hermetically sealing itself."[16] Andy used it to cook their biscuits that night, but they left the remainder of the sack behind.

Two days were spent in portaging and lining Disaster Falls—"No boat could go through it," Thompson observed—and it was 24 June before they were able to resume their voyage. They ran rapid after rapid until they came to one at the base of the romantically named Cliff of the Harp, which they decided to line. Here they found more pieces of the *No Name*, including an axe, a vise, and a copy of *Putnams Magazine*. Triplet Falls lay just downstream, and when he saw the long portage they would have to make to get past it, Clem lamented, "Oh me, but there is a long, weary portage to make tomorrow of about a mile long."[17] Nor were their troubles over, for only one-half mile below Triplet lay Hell's Half Mile, Lodore's worst rapid. The proper Prof Thompson and Beaman were inclined toward "Boulder Falls" as a name for this maelstrom of rocks and water. Powell, however, asked Steward what he thought it should be named and Steward immediately replied, "Will Hell's Half Mile suit?" and the rapid was so christened.[18] The men had good reason to curse this rapid, for they had to build a trail above it and haul their tons of supplies around it on their backs, and then line the boats down to calmer water. After two days of work, hauling load after load of supplies, and standing in cold, rushing water, the men felt that Hell's Half Mile had more than earned its name.

Just after they finished portaging Hell's Half Mile, they had an experience similar to what the first party had faced, at almost the same place, when their breakfast fire spread into the surrounding brush and set it ablaze. Hillers noted that "the dense smoke rolled up to the peaks some 2800 ft in height and then out of 'Lodore'."[19] Some of the men were up on the cliffs above camp taking readings when they saw smoke. They hurried back to camp just in time to save their boats and supplies.

With the rocks and rapids and portages and fires, it is little wonder they were glad to see the end of the canyon. "We are through with Lodore with its rapids, its reminisences of disaster, its hard work and danger," the usually taciturn Thompson exulted. "It is as a tale that is past. We fear it no more, we rejoice; nine days only to run it. Three portages. No disaster."[20] On the twenty-fifth, after stops at Rippling Brook and Alcove Brook, they ran the last few miles into Echo Park. Here they were to stay for about a week, and the men were glad of the respite. The boats needed to be recalked, their clothes needed repairs, and the scientific work needed to be recorded. The Major, however, was not one to sit idle, so on the twenty-seventh he took Jones, Beaman, Hattan, and Hillers up the Yampa in the *Emma Dean* to survey the tributary as far up from its mouth as they could row.

Meanwhile, Steward and Clem Powell decided to walk back up Lodore to measure the height of the cliffs near its mouth. They were gone all day and late into the night. The others were beginning to worry, when the hapless pair finally stumbled back into camp wet, bedraggled, exhausted, embarrassed, and quite reluctant at first to tell what had happened. After some prodding from Dellenbaugh, though, they sheepishly confessed they had almost drowned through foolishness. Rather than risk climbing back in the dark, they decided to float down to Echo Park on a raft made of dead junipers. Although there are no rapids at that point, the river is very swift, and the raft was soon torn apart by the strong currents. Both were sucked into a whirlpool and came close to losing their lives. Steward and Clem begged Dellenbaugh not to reveal their error to the Major, but just then Thompson came up to the fire and demanded to know what had happened. "Their punishment for this indiscretion," Dellenbaugh concludes, "was a hard climb back to where they had left a rifle and other things that must be recovered."[21]

Aside from this little "indiscretion," the week spent in Echo Park was enjoyable. There was time to rest their weary muscles away from the roaring rapids, to listen to the wind and the birds chirping in the groves of trees, time to swim in the calm river. One night while the Major was still gone, the others took a moonlight row up the Yampa and made the walls echo with song. Dellenbaugh, writing of the night many years later, still remembered the evening as "one of the fairest pictures I have ever seen."

On 30 June, Thompson, Steward, and Bishop floated down to the lower end of Echo Park and climbed out Pool Creek Canyon—they called it Steward's Creek—to the top of a point now known as Harper's Corner. From there they had a magnificent view of Whirlpool Canyon, the mountains surrounding Lodore, Island Park, and Jones Hole. Looking up the Yampa, they could see the Major returning, the distant boat looking like a "waterbug." The climbers hurried back to camp, arriving about the same time as the weary and hungry men who had accompanied Powell.

The latter had rowed up the Yampa a few miles without much trouble, but had then come to a small rapid, which took them three tries and a lot of hard work to get past. They spent four days exploring the side canyons and parks of the lower Yampa. On the thirtieth, with provisions running low, they returned to Echo Park, having traveled about twelve miles upriver. They were very glad to get back to camp, and after a hearty supper, Hillers says, "the evening was spent in telling adventures."

The crew stayed in Echo Park for a few more days, but on 3 July it was time to move on. They ran a couple of little rapids in Whirlpool Canyon, portaged another, and camped that night in the charming wooded glen named Jones Hole.[22] The Major declared a holiday on the Fourth of July, and they celebrated the occasion with a shot from their rifles for every state in the union. Dellenbaugh, who was cook for the day, concocted a grand feast of ham, pie, stewed apples, canned peaches, bread, coffee and tea, and candy. The canned peaches were brought by Hillers and the candy by young Fred. Both had secretly obtained the delicacies in Green River and saved them for just this event.[23] After supper, Hillers concludes, "[we] lit our pipes and cursed the Irish until it was time to seek the fond embrace of Morpheus, and so ended the glorious fourth of July of 1871."[24]

"Not having the usual means of celebration, we awoke the next morning in good working condition, and making fair progress, arrived the same evening in Island Park."[25] So Beaman lightly passes off the rest of Whirlpool Canyon, although some of the others mention running three rapids and lining another. By midafternoon they were drifting through the quiet meanders of Island Park. They camped that night at the head of what Major Powell had called Craggy Canyon on his last trip, but was now called Split Mountain Canyon.

Powell decided to push on ahead of the party to reach the Uinta Ute Agency. He wanted to make sure that everything was still going according to plan and that they would have replacement provisions when they got to the mouth of the Uinta River. Taking Hillers, Bishop, and Jones in the *Emma Dean,* he left early on the morning of 7 July. After three days of hard rowing through the flat water of the Uinta Basin, they reached their destination. They had covered eighty river miles, all but eight of that without any current to speak of, and still had a twenty-mile walk to reach the agency. When they finally trudged up to the agency the next day, the Major learned that Jacob Hamblin had been unsuccessful in his attempt to reach the mouth of the Dirty Devil River, their next scheduled rendezvous for provisions. On hearing this news, the Major left for Salt Lake City that same day to solve the problem, leaving word for the others to wait at the mouth of the Uinta for further instructions.

The men at the head of Split Mountain Canyon, of course, knew nothing of any of these developments. They made their way in a leisurely manner through the canyon, stopping frequently for Beaman to take photographs, collecting fossils, and enjoying the warm, mosquito-free days. At one point they saw a flock of mountain sheep, and fired volley after volley at them—"Had quite an engagement," Thompson remarks—but failed to hit any. They reached the foot of the canyon on 11 July, about the same time that the other half of their party was traveling up the dusty road to the Ute agency.

The night of the thirteenth was a restless one. Signs of Indians were all about, and that made all of them except the imperturbable Thompson uneasy. Some of the men did not like having the party divided, and campfire talk was of all the disasters that could have befallen the others. Steward, in particular, "croaked for an hour." Early that morning they were suddenly awakened by a huge limb that came crashing down out of one of the cottonwood trees. That seemed to break the tension, and all (except Steward) relaxed.

On the river, the crew reached what seemed to be the appointed meeting place and found no sign of the Major or their companions, even though they searched all that day. The men began to grow uneasy again. Thompson was becoming disgusted with them: "The croakers are as usual full of forebodings. The boys are killed. Everything bad has happened. . . . I am going to sleep. Shall find traces of them in the morning, I think."[26] The next morning they discovered that they had indeed gone past the correct spot and they rowed back upriver. After some searching they found a note from the Major in a tin can. Later that evening, they heard signal shots, and soon Bishop and Jones came riding into camp with some unsettling news for their companions. Critchlow, the Indian agent, had left strict instructions that his men were not to help Powell's party in any way. The crew was faced with the prospect of packing provisions down to the river on their backs until Mr. Basor, the trader at the agency, furnished them with a team and a wagon and helped them haul their supplies down to the boats. The other bad news was about the Major. He had deemed it necessary to go himself and find a route into the mouth of the Dirty Devil or some other spot where they could be reprovisioned. They would have to face Desolation Canyon without him.

After a stay of almost a month at the camp near the mouth of the Uinta River, the party resumed their journey on 5 August. They passed through Desolation and Gray canyons without mishap, and after another long wait at the old Spanish crossing they were rejoined by the Major on the twenty-ninth. For the rest of their trip on the Green, through the calm and beautiful Labyrinth and Stillwater canyons, they were able to float along with the boats lashed together, listening to the Major read poetry. By the middle of September, however, they were back to portaging and lining. It took them ten days to get through Cataract Canyon, and they did not reach the rations that Powell had left at the Crossing of the Fathers in Glen Canyon until the end of the month. There the Major decided to end the river journey for the year and cache the boats. They would return the next year and complete the river survey. In the meantime, the crew would work on surveying and mapping the Kaibab Plateau and the region around the Grand Canyon.

Beaman, Steward, and Bishop would not be part of the crew for the last leg of the river journey, however. Beaman left because of a personality clash with the Major, and the latter two because of failing health. Of the remainder, Clem Powell and Dellenbaugh worked through the winter and then were on hand for the trip through the Grand Canyon. Hillers, who had by this time become the expedition's photographer, Jones, Thompson, and Hattan were also along. The spring run-off was unusually high, and thinking no doubt of the perilous rapids he knew were to come, the Major decided to terminate the river survey at Kanab Creek, about halfway through the Grand Canyon. Only Hillers and Thompson stayed on with the Major after another field season and continued their work when the survey was incorporated into the newly formed U.S. Geological Survey in 1879.

It is one of those strange quirks of history that even though the second Powell survey of the river is well documented in both human and scientific terms, it remains virtually unknown today except in the vaguest sense.[27] The impact of the hardworking and loyal crew's explorations of the rivers and the surrounding country, however, cannot be overstated. Places of mystery and legend were, as a result of Powell's surveys, exposed to science and the public eye. The canyons were mapped, the cliffs measured, the fall of the river plotted. There was still plenty of unknown land around the river, but the canyons themselves were now known. After Powell, great changes began to take place both on the lands around the river and on the river itself. Whether these changes were just part of the overall settlement of the West or a direct result of Powell's surveys, or both, is a matter for scholars to debate. However, the Green River would never be the same.

6

Revolution on the River

"Men live rich and quiet lives outside the boiling currents of their times, and who shall say whether the thousand existences in quiet do not more nearly express the shape of human experience than the fiercely spotlighted existence that survives as history?"[1] When western historian Dale Morgan posed this question in his book on the Great Salt Lake, he could just as easily have been referring to the Green River. The "boiling currents" of the last third of the nineteenth century completely bypassed the remote canyons of the upper Green. There was little mention of the river in newspapers, and no brave expeditions pushed off from Green River City to the cheers of the townspeople. And yet even though these last three decades were quiet in terms of world-shaking events, to the river and to the river environment they were important and even revolutionary years.

The empty lands the early explorers had floated through were gone. People were beginning to move into the bottomlands and valleys along the river to settle, to start ranches and farms, to build towns. Between 1870 and 1900, small towns sprang up. Green River City, Wyoming, went from a hell-on-wheels, end-of-the-line railroad town to a settled community with a church, a school, and even a newspaper. Downstream, there was Linwood, just over the Utah line; Bridgeport and Lodore in Browns Park, which were post offices if not towns, and indicative of the growing population in that remote valley; and Jensen and Vernal in the Uinta Basin. The former was located on the river, and the latter not far from it. By 1900 both were thriving towns. In between were a number of prosperous ranches, many of them around Linwood and Manila, an area that was so fertile it came to be known as Lucerne Valley. Other ranches included the Chew place on Pool Creek near Echo Park, and the Ruple Ranch in Island Park, later to become a favorite stop for river runners.

Since people lived by the river, they needed to get across it. Quite a few ferries began operation and even a few bridges were built. There was the railroad bridge at Green River, of course, and below that the Brinnegar Ferry near Linwood. John Jarvie had a ferry at the upper end of Browns Park, and just downstream there was Charlie Crouse's short-lived bridge at Bridgeport.[2] There were also the Alhandra Ferry and the Maube Ferry near Jensen, in the Uinta Basin, which operated until put out of business by the new bridge built at Jensen in 1911.[3]

The real changes of these years, however, took place on the river itself. There had been a wide variety of craft used in the attempts to navigate the river. The canyons had witnessed Ashley in his bullboats, Manly in his ferryboat and dugout canoes, and finally Major Powell in his heavy oak rowboats. About the only things any of them had in common were that they floated and that almost all of them failed to negotiate the rapids safely and successfully.

Around the middle of the 1880s, a trapper and sometime prospector from Vernal named Nathaniel Galloway decided that there were beaver aplenty in the canyons of the Green and maybe gold as well. He wanted to get into the canyons to reap the rich harvest he knew was waiting there, but moreover, he wanted to get home again. He had probably heard of Powell's boats and his barely successful passage of the canyons above Vernal from that other part-time resident of Vernal, Frank Goodman, and so he decided to build his own boat. No one knows just where he got the idea for the design, but his results speak for themselves. The "Galloway boat," as it was called, was a flat-bottomed skiff, broad at the stern, which was usually about fourteen or fifteen feet long and four feet wide. It weighed about four hundred pounds, quite a bit less than the Major's freight boats. Galloway's boats had a pronounced rake, or rise, fore and aft. Some were open, but most had some sort of decking of wood or canvas fore and aft, leaving a cockpit for the oarsman.[4] He built his boats of wood, although he did

Linwood, Utah, August 1917.

experiment with canvas once. It was not successful, as he wrote to Julius Stone in 1910: "I runn the canyons this fawl with a canvas folding boat and it kept me patching punctures all the way through." Galloway built his boats for one. Unless a person was small enough to huddle on the floor of the cockpit, a passenger had to sit on or cling to the rear deck, which may explain why so many early passengers decided to walk around rapids. It didn't make much difference to Galloway, for he almost always went by himself.

Not only did Galloway design and build his own boats, he used them in an entirely different manner. There are two ways to control a boat in rough water: go faster than the current, like a canoe or a motorboat, or slower. Major Powell was actually the first to give serious consideration to the problem of navigating rapids, and unfortunately for his crews, he chose the former method. His boats were built sturdily enough to withstand the shock of hitting rocks in the channel, but as a result, they were extraordinarily heavy and clumsy. When he realized that they were still not strong enough to withstand constant pounding, he chose to line or portage most rapids, much to the disgust of his men. They in fact ended up spending more time lining and portaging rapids than they did running them.[5] When they did run rapids, they careened headlong down the channel, the two oarsmen rowing for all they were worth, while the steersman tried to provide some measure of control with the steering oar and shouted orders to the others. Besides being rather unnerving for the men, who couldn't see where they were rowing, this method left almost no time to maneuver. Mishaps and even wrecks were almost inevitable.

Galloway changed all that, by the simple expedient of turning his boat around and facing downstream. This solved a number of problems at once. Most simply, it allowed him to see where he was going. Equally important, he could slow the boat down on the approach to a rapid, or even in the midst of one, so that he could recognize obstacles in time to avoid them. He didn't have to depend on a steersman for directions, whose orders could never be heard above the roar of the rapid anyway. Galloway's flat-bottomed, highly maneuverable boat could turn on a proverbial dime and even hover in the midst of a churning rapid. With this setup, Than Galloway, as his friends called him, was ready to deal with the rapids of the Green.[6]

Galloway's first known trip on the Green was in 1891, but aside from the bare fact that he went, little is known about this voyage. It is fairly certain that he had gone before then, but no record exists. He made five more runs of the Green between 1891 and 1895, but aside from brief articles in the *Vernal Express,* little detail has survived. There is always the possibility that on some of his trips he did a little illegal trapping—as others of the time were doing—which might account for the lack of records. Most likely, though, he was just too busy running his boat to keep any sort of diary.[7]

A run he made in the fall of 1895 is the first about which a definite record exists. He and a partner started from Green River, Wyoming, and went all the way down the Green to its confluence with the Grand, and then back upstream to Moab, Utah. The next spring they started to repeat the same trip, but went only as far as Nine Mile Creek at the head of Desolation Canyon.[8]

Galloway's first well-documented trip was made in the autumn of 1898.[9] He and his thirteen-year-old son, John, started from the mouth of Henry's Fork with the intention of trapping their way down the river. In Red Canyon, they met William Richmond and his partner, Frank Leland, a pair of hard-luck prospectors. These two had started out from the same place as the Galloways a few days before in a homemade boat, towing a placer-mining outfit on a crude raft. They planned to try their luck in the sandbars of the Green, but made it only as far as Ashley Falls. Richmond didn't like the idea of unloading the whole outfit and hauling it on their backs around the rapid, so he tried to run it. This cost them dearly, for the river claimed the entire mining apparatus, and almost got their small boat with all their supplies and gear. It was a forlorn pair of prospectors that the Galloways found in Little Hole that night.

Around their campfire, Galloway proposed that they join forces and go all the way through the Grand Canyon. There was plenty of trapping to do along the way, and there had been rumors of possible color in the sandbars in Glen Canyon. Richmond thought that a fine idea, but his partner had seen enough of the river. Leland took their dog and walked out of the canyon the next day, headed for Rock Springs.

The Galloways and Richmond continued down the river. In Lodore they ran all of the rapids except Lower Disaster Falls and Hell's Half Mile. When they reached Jensen, they dropped off young John at his mother's. At Nine Mile Creek they switched over to the boats that Nathaniel had stored there the year before and went all the way through the Grand Canyon, arriving in Needles, California, in February 1899.

Later that same year, Galloway was once again cruising the canyons, trapping all the way down the river to Lee's Ferry at the end of Glen Canyon. He arrived at Lee's Ferry in October and spent the rest of the year working as a boatman for Robert Brewster Stanton, the engineer for the ill-fated Hoskaninni Mining Company. This oufit, financed by a millionaire from Ohio named Julius Stone, was trying to extract the fine gold from the sands of Glen Canyon with a huge placer dredge that cost over $300,000. It was notably unsuccessful. On a couple of occasions, though, Galloway guided Stone through the canyon, and they went hunting in the Henry Mountains. The friendship that grew out of this association was to have important consequences for both of them.

By 1901 Galloway was back on the upper Green. That year he started at Meeker, Colorado, trapped down the White River to its confluence with the Green, and then followed the main stream to Green River, Utah. In 1903 Galloway introduced his other son, Parley, to the river with a trip on the Green from Vernal to the confluence and back up to Moab. He followed another trip down the White with a run from Desolation Canyon to Lee's Ferry. September of 1905 found Galloway once again around the upper Green, where he stayed until 1908, when he tested a new design, a steel boat, on a trip from Green River, Wyoming, to Green River, Utah. How this design worked out he never said, but when he went down the Yampa River with Parley in the spring of 1909, he was back in a wooden boat.[10]

In September of that year Galloway began what is without doubt his best-known trip, with his old employer, Julius Stone. Since he floated Glen Canyon with Galloway back in 1899, Stone had been toying with the idea of a traverse of all the canyons of the Green and Colorado. Just after that experience, he had read Powell's report, and intrigued by the idea of running the entire river, had gone to see the aging Major at his office in Washington, D.C. Powell was not very friendly and was possessive in his attitude about the river—he had done it, but no one else could possibly duplicate his feat. A bit insulted by the gruff Powell, Stone decided to go and see the river for himself. He recalled Galloway's expertise on the river, and hired him as expedition guide. He also brought Galloway back to Ohio to supervise the building of the boats to be used on the trip.[11]

On the afternoon of Sunday, 12 September 1909, the Galloway–Stone party left Green River, Wyoming. Mr. Morris, who had let them use his barn to organize their gear, gave Stone a bottle of rye whiskey in case one of them had an accident and might need a general anesthetic. When Stone wrote his account of the trip almost a quarter of a century later, he was proud to say that he still had the unopened bottle.[12]

By the seventeenth, they had passed through the first three canyons on the upper Green. Stone and Galloway each rowed a boat. C. C. Sharp, another member of the party, rowed another, while Seymour Dubendorff, a friend of Galloway's from Myton, Utah, whom Stone described as "gritty as a flapjack rolled in sand," rowed the last boat. Raymond Cogswell, the expedition's photographer and Stone's brother-in-law, rode with "Dubie" in the last boat. At Ashley Falls, Galloway ran three of the boats through, but Stone rowed his own. He almost collided with Galloway in the midst of the falls when Stone pulled an oar out of its lock at the head of the rapid, but the more experienced boatman was able to avoid a collision. They stopped below the falls to look for Ashley's inscription, but were unable to locate it.[13]

On the morning of the nineteenth, they ran Red Creek Rapid at the end of Red Canyon, and at noon they came into Browns Park and passed the abandoned ranch of John Jarvie, an early settler of the park, who had been murdered by two itinerant laborers from Rock Springs only two months before.[14] They floated quickly through the open valley, reaching the Gates of Lodore on Tuesday the twenty-first. Stone and his crew stopped to visit with some engineers from the U.S. Reclamation Service, whose camp they found at the head of the canyon. The engineers were testing the riverbed for damsites, but no one was home except the cook, so they continued on into Lodore. About two miles below Winnie's Rapid, they passed the damsite drilling crew, who did not seem to be having much luck finding suitable bedrock.

The next morning they came to Disaster Falls. The men portaged half their supplies around the rapid, but on closer examination, Galloway decided to run the boats and the remaining provisions through. They were past the rapid by midafternoon. Stone commented, somewhat smugly: "This is the rapid where one of Powell's boats was wrecked and lost. The illustration shown of Disaster Falls [in Powell's report] is inexcusably innaccurate. This is not a "fall" in any sense whatever, and should not be so named."[15]

Camp that night was at Pot Creek, about halfway through the canyon. Stone showed in his journal entry for the day that he was as much impressed with the quieter side of the canyon as he was with the rapids: "The sky is beautifully opalescent in the north since sunset. The cliff on the east side glows in rich vermilion under the reflected light of the sky."[16]

They slept late the next morning, "being somewhat worn out with yesterday's efforts." Their labors were just beginning, however, as the itinerary for the day included Triplet Falls and Hell's Half Mile. At the former, Galloway ran all the boats through himself, one at a time. Stone, who was proving to be a good boatman in his own right, was somewhat miffed that Galloway was having all the fun, while he and the rest of the men lugged the baggage and provisions past the steep cliffs and boulders.

> I do not quite understand his hesitation about letting each one handle his own boat, unless it is because of his unqualified confidence in himself. He and I have been together a good deal, and this is the first time he has ever assumed any attitude of guardianship. Heretofore he has always taken it as a matter of course that I would do my share and look out for myself.[17]

Just downstream was Hell's Half Mile. They looked it over and decided there were too many rocks and not enough water, so they hauled the boats out of the river and portaged them over the slippery rocks past the worst part of the rapid. While doing this they discovered that rocks and rushing water were not the only dangers they faced in the canyon.

> [W]e have to climb a high talus on the right side that is lying barely at the angle of repose and starts to slide at the slightest provocation. It is interspersed with various low-growing cacti. . . . Sharp, in trying to save himself from slipping with the sliding rock, unfortunately sits down on one of these bunches. He never swears, but I am sure he now realizes the painful limitations of a wholly polite vocabulary.[18]

The next morning, after a cold camp and no supper, they were no doubt happy to see the end of Lodore. They didn't linger long in Echo Park, however, and after lunch under the box elder trees, floated on down Whirlpool Canyon to Jones Hole and an early camp. Galloway went fishing after camp was set up and came back with thirty-one fine trout. It was a good supper and a good camp. They were glad to be out of Lodore, and everyone, Stone wrote at the end of the day, was "as happy and full of good spirits—and trout—as he can be."

They stayed late the next day. While the others went hunting and fishing, Stone decided to spend the day in camp,

> to patch my trousers, luxuriating in the sunshine and comfort of the day. . . . The autumn colors in the trees are softened by the pale green of the rabbit brush, here and there breaking into sprays of golden blossoms. Beneath them grow low yellow and purple flowers. And all blend into a harmony strangely in keeping with the ruggedness of the canyon walls and the restless, hurrying water that plays so rough and yet so fair a game.
>
> The note of a bluebird comes intermittently from the thicket that fringes the river's lip, while the sun creeps around the rim of the crag that hides it nearly all the time. I see a water ouzel in the creek and afterward hear him in the thicket.[19]

After passing through the rest of Whirlpool Canyon, they camped in Island Park and met Art Ruple, one of the many settlers who had moved into the area since the turn of the century. The boaters put Split Mountain behind them the next day without mishap, although they had to portage their supplies at one point, probably Moonshine Rapid, and had a near-miss in Inglesby Rapid, near the end of the canyon.

The next day everyone was up early, as they wanted to reach Vernal by sundown. On the way, they passed the newly discovered beds of dinosaur fossils above Jensen, and Galloway told the others about the Carnegie Museum crew who had been there for the past couple of years.[20] The weary men reached Vernal late that night and immediately checked into a hotel, glad for the chance to sleep in a bed for the first time in almost a month. They stayed in Vernal for two days. Galloway and Dubendorff visited their families, while Stone and the others did some shopping for necessary supplies, tools, and so on, and also took the time to get acquainted with the country and some of the residents of Ashley Valley. By the last day of September, however, they were ready to leave, and departed after a big picnic lunch given by the local residents.

Stone and his men finished their voyage at Needles, California, on 19 November 1909, having made the entire trip in just over five weeks. The most important point to make about Julius Stone's voyage, however, was not the time it took, or the boats, or the fact that this was one of Nathaniel Galloway's last trips down any river.[21] It was, rather, the motivation. Ostensibly, he went down the river to photograph the

canyons and check up on Major Powell, but the real reason was much
more basic. It was adventure, pure and simple. Stone went just because
he wanted to. The "Wild West" era of American history was ending;
most of the Indians were on reservations, the buffalo were gone, the
vast distances shortened by the railroads. For the first time, river travelers
went down the Green not for gold, or furs, or science, but for adventure. The canyons of the Green were one of the places left in the West
where wilderness still existed, where adventure was still possible. The
river had become a last frontier.

It was barely two years before more travelers responded to the call
of the river and the rapids. Ellsworth and Emery Kolb and a young
man they hired as camp help, James Fagan, arrived in Green River,
Wyoming, to follow Stone. Ellsworth had in fact applied to Stone to
be photographer for his trip, but Cogswell had already been selected.
In 1901 the brothers had opened a photography studio on the south rim
of the Grand Canyon, and since then had made their living selling scenic photographs to the thousands of tourists who flocked to see the canyon. They had another ambition, however, as Ellsworth described at
the beginning of the book he later wrote about their journey: they wanted
to "make the 'Big Trip' . . . and secure a pictorial record of the entire
series of canyons on the Green and Colorado Rivers." Furthermore,
he said later, they wanted to do it themselves, without a guide. Photographs or not, the two brothers were really after the same thing that
Stone had been—adventure.

After getting Stone's advice, the Kolbs built their boats according
to the proven Galloway design. They started at the same time of the
year as Stone, in September when the water was lower and therefore
slower. An important difference, however, was the fact that neither of
the brothers had ever rowed a boat through any sort of rapids before,
nor had the young Jimmy Fagan, who was along just for the ride. This
lack of experience, in Otis Marston's dry phrase, "insured adventure."
Another thing they had no control over was the weather. They were
not to enjoy the warm days and cool nights that had so pleased Julius
Stone two years before. For most of the trip they had to endure what
Ellsworth called "Wyoming weather": wind, rain, and thunderstorms.

They started on 8 September 1911.[22] The brothers had already made
sure their cameras—8-x-10 and 5-x-7 view cameras, and an innovation

on the river, a movie camera—were in order, well packed and water-proofed. They had done their last-minute shopping for supplies, and endured the visits of the townspeople, "not one of [whom]," Ellsworth commented in *Through the Grand Canyon,* "had any encouragement to offer." They were relieved to cast off into the river, which was lower for this time of year than anyone could remember.

The low water didn't bother them a bit, however. They spent six easy days covering the sixty miles to Flaming Gorge. They stopped here and there at the ranches along the way to visit with the families and get fresh provisions, and were surprised to find that the ideas people had about the river here, closer to the canyons, were markedly different from those of the inhabitants of Green River. "There were comments by some of the men on our venture, but they lacked the true Green River tang. Here, close to the upper canyons, the unreasonable fear of the rapids gave way to a reasonable respect for them."[23]

The Kolbs practiced rowing their new boats through the fast waters of Flaming Gorge, Kingfisher, and Horseshoe canyons, in order to get the feel of the craft before the heavier and more difficult rapids of Red Canyon and beyond. When they started into the latter canyon, however, it was the low water that caused the most problems. "Too many rocks, not enough water," Ellsworth recorded succinctly. Still, the rocky rapids were good practice, and it was better than going in June, when the spring flood changed the river into wild, uncontrollable fury. Their rowing skills began to show gradual improvement.

On the nineteenth they reached Ashley Falls and ran their boats through the chute with only a couple of knocks. In honor of the successful passage of their first known rapid, they christened their boats that night. Emery called his the *Edith,* after his wife, while the unmarried Ellsworth called his melodramatically, the *Defiance.* Back on the river, near a place appropriately named Outlaw Flat, they encountered a man who had a ranch near the canyon bottom. He sold them some food, and in return for this favor they helped him to herd some horses across the river. Soon after this, however, the man began to act suspicious of the trio of river runners and questioned them closely as to their reason for being in that remote mountain country. The brothers had heard tales of rustlers and outlaws living in that part of the mountains and were probably more than a little relieved to be on their way. They learned from some honest ranchers in Browns Park that their suspicions about the man had been correct.

A tense moment in Ashley Falls for Emery Kolb in 1911.

Our former host, we were told, had committed many depredations and had served one term for cattle stealing. . . . [Our] cool welcome, their suspicions of us, the sinister arsenal of guns and pistols, all was explained! Quite likely some of these weapons had been trained against us . . . on the chance that we were either officers of the law, or competitors in the horse-stealing industry. For that matter we were actually guilty of the latter count, for come to think of it, we had helped them steal eight horses and a colt![24]

After spending four pleasant days floating through Browns Park, they camped at the Gates of Lodore. "This twenty-mile canyon," Ellsworth wrote that night, "bears a very unsavory reputation, having a fall of 425 feet in that short distance. . . . This would mean wild water somewhere!" This soon proved to be the case; after running four little rapids they came to Winnie's Rapid, which looked too dangerous to try. Emery's boat was soon lined down, but that proved to be too much work, so Ellsworth ran the *Defiance* through the rapid, while Emery recorded the event from shore with the movie camera. When the latter jokingly said that Ellsworth should have capsized to make it a better picture, the other brother commented, "I refused to upset even to please my brother."[25]

They ran the rest of the small rapids down to Disaster Falls, and after looking at the upper part of that famous rapid, decided it could be run as well. Lower Disaster Falls, where the river is split by a rocky island and sweeps under an overhanging cliff, was not to be so easily passed, so they lined the boats along the left side of the river. So far, Lodore had proven to be no worse than Red Canyon, and they began to feel confident in their boats and their new-found skills. "Pride goeth before the fall," Ellsworth ruefully recorded, and just below Disaster Falls the *Edith* ran up on a rock and swamped. Soon after that mishap, Ellsworth suffered the same experience in the *Defiance,* but in his case the boat received a severe blow to the stern. Everything in both boats was wet, including the cameras. An early camp was made, and the brothers set about drying their gear, taking special care with the delicate camera mechanisms. "It was a night long to be remembered," Ellsworth wrote, and for more than just the day's events on the river.

> It rained again in torrents, and the wind howled about the tent. After midnight, as we still toiled, a land-slide, loosened by the soaking rains, thundered down the mountain side about a fourth of a mile below our camp. . . . Smaller slides followed at intervals, descending over the 3000-foot precipices. Thunder reverberated through the canyon. . . . These slides made one feel a little uncomfortable.[26]

Repairs to the *Defiance* took them the better part of two days, and it was the morning of the twenty-ninth before they could resume their journey. They had gone only a short distance when they came to Triplet Falls, and after the experiences of the last few days they decided not to take any chances. For the rest of the day, they portaged their gear and lined one boat past the rapid. That night they were repaid for their labors with an idyllic campsite, plenty of wood, and a smooth sandy beach to sleep on just at the foot of the rapid. There they enjoyed the first peaceful night's sleep in what seemed like ages.

They needed the rest, as it turned out, for just below Triplet lay Hell's Half Mile. "Our previous work was as nothing to this," they lamented. The rounded boulders next to the rapid were covered with slimy mud from the recent rains, which made the backbreaking work of moving the boats along the side of the river that much harder. Then there were supplies, bedrolls, camera gear, and other equipment to be carried past the falls. Nine loads were needed to empty one boat; each load had to be carried three hundred feet up the side of the canyon to get past the cliffs and back down to the river. It was the end of the day before their boats were past the rapid and floating in the quiet waters below.

They were not sorry to see the end of Lodore the next day. On 2 October, camped in Echo Park, Ellsworth summed up their impressions of the Canyon of Lodore:

> No doubt it was a beautiful and a wonderful place, but none of us seemed sorry to leave it behind. For ten days we had not had a single day entirely free from rain, and instead of having a chance to run rapids it seemed as if we had spent an entire week in carrying our loads, or in lining our boats through the canyon.[27]

The openness and quiet of Echo Park was a welcome balm to their tense nerves and sore muscles, and they made the most of it. They camped near the mouth of Pool Creek, and Emery and Fagan set off up the creek that evening to see if they could find the Chew Ranch, which was reported to be near Echo Park. They had all agreed the night before that they would see if the Chews could provide transportation for Fagan to get back to civilization. He had seen enough of the river, the rain, and the rockslides, and was homesick besides. On reaching the ranch, they found Mrs. Chew at home, and, much to the younger man's relief, she agreed to take him along when she went over the mountain to Vernal two days hence.

The Chews invited the river travelers to dinner the next day, and Mr. Chew treated them to stories about life in the remote country around Browns Park. He had been the one to discover the body of poor John Jarvie, which had been thrown in a skiff and cast adrift on the river, and was "all swelled up like a toad" when found.[28] Furthermore, he often found the carcasses of his horses and cattle, which had been killed by outlaws trying to drive an honest rancher like himself out of the country.

As they were listening to Mr. Chew's tales, up rode one of the most interesting characters ever to inhabit the canyon country. Pat Lynch had lived in various caves and shacks around the Green and the Yampa since the 1870s.[29] He was a big man with wild gray hair who spoke with a slight Irish burr. No one every really knew what his background was, but as he told it, he had run away to sea at an early age and had been shipwrecked on the west coast of Africa. There he had been adopted by a tribe of cannibals, who had even favored him with a wife. He escaped from them after a few years and joined the U.S. Navy just in time to serve in the Civil War. After being wounded in a naval battle in 1863, he had been mustered out of the service, but soon enlisted in the U.S. Army Quartermaster Corps under the name James Cooper. He was in and out of the army until 1870, when he left the military for good and settled in Colorado.

Pat soon drifted into the wild, uninhabited country around the Yampa and lived there as a hermit the rest of his life. He kept a herd of fine horses that he was very proud of, and he would sometimes sell or trade one of them to the outlaws who used the trails running south from Browns Park. His other sources of income were two military pensions that he drew, one under each name! Not that he needed much in the way of material goods or food, however. According to F. C. Barnes, the postmaster at Lily Park, Colorado, and a long-time friend of Pat's,

> [he] lived just like a coyote. If he found a dead horse, he would take a quarter or a half and make jerky out of it. This is the kind of meat he always kept on hand. I have known him to take a drowned horse out of the river and make jerky out of it. He had jerky and bread cached all over the mountains. I have been riding with him on different trips. He would stop and study for a minute, then turn to one side and go to a rock or cleft and get some meat and bread. The meat was always jerky and the bread looked like it might have been cooked a year or more.[30]

Pat spent most of his time visiting his friends up and down the river, and was a frequent caller at the Chew Ranch on Pool Creek. Ralph Chew, who as a boy knew Pat quite well, recalls that whenever anyone would mention the death of a local resident, Pat would cock his head and ask if the victim had been killed with an axe. It seems that one of the many explanations of Pat's hermit lifestyle was that he had killed someone with an axe back east and was hiding out from the law.[31] Pat also often visited the Ruples in Island Park. When he wanted to pay them a call, he would float downriver from his little ranch in Echo Park, holding onto a log. At the end of the visit, he would borrow a horse from Art Ruple and ride back. Once he was home, he would turn the horse loose, give it a slap on the rump, and the horse would find its own way home.

Pat was almost deaf, but that didn't stop him from conversing with the animals who shared his canyon home. He swore that there was a mountain lion near one of his caves that would answer when he called, and it was true that no animal was afraid in his presence. Besides the animals, he "had a way of conversing with spirits" that could be disconcerting to those not accustomed to his ways. Pat made quite the impression on the Kolb brothers, but they found the acquaintance frustrating as well.

> He was so old that he scarecely knew what he was talking about, rambling from one subject to another; and would have us listening with impatience to hear the end of some wonderful tale of the early days, when he would suddenly switch off to an entirely different subject, leaving the first unfinished.[32]

The last few years of his life Pat grew too feeble to live by himself, so he stayed with his friend Barnes in Lily Park. It is reported that his last wish was to be set adrift on the river he had lived by for so long, but when he died on 27 February 1917, he was buried next to the Yampa in Lily Park, where a weathered stone still marks his grave.

After their memorable dinner, the Kolbs and Jimmy Fagan parted company. Fagan rode out to Vernal in the back of a two-wheeled cart with Mrs. Chew and son Ralph,[33] while the Kolbs returned to their boats. They were relaxed and confident the next day as they continued their journey on the river.

> [W]ith one less man and considerably less baggage as well, [the boats] were lighter by far. Our chances looked much more favourable for an easy passage. Not only were these things in our favour, but in addition we felt that we had served our apprenticeship at navigation in rapid water, and we were just as capable of meeting the rapids to follow as if we had years of experience to our record.[34]

Their confidence was justified, it would seem; they ran all of the rapids in Whirlpool Canyon in less than three hours. Chafing at the slow miles through Island Park, Ellsworth complained that "nine miles of rowing brought us back to a point about three miles from the mouth of Whirlpool Canyon," a complaint shared, incidentally, by many modern river runners. If it was excitement they wanted, however, it was not long in coming. Split Mountain Canyon proved to be a real challenge, and they likened its rapids to the ones they had seen in their travels along the bottom of the Grand Canyon. They barely avoided an upset in Moonshine Rapid, and when they camped just above the end of the canyon that night they decided that it had been a very full day.

They floated the rest of the canyon in a couple of hours the next morning. Seven miles of hard rowing brought them to a placer dredge on the side of the river. Anxious to check on the films they had sent out with Mrs. Chew, they landed to see if they could find out how far it was to Jensen. There was no one at camp except a "sleek, well-fed cat," but they did find a telephone. A call to the operator let them know that they had nine miles to go. Another few hours of hard rowing brought them to the little town, where they spent the night.

During the ride to Vernal on two "spirited" horses the next day, the brothers were very impressed with the beautiful Ashley Valley. Ellsworth commented on the lush orchards and fields and the orderly ranches "laid out in true Mormon style . . . squared off in sections, fenced, and planted with shade trees. . . ." They hoped to meet the "old man of the river," Nathaniel Galloway, but they were disappointed to find that he was up on the mountain on a hunting trip. When they reached Vernal, one of the first things they noticed was a group of men gathered around young Fagan, who had reached the town just a few hours before them, and was thrilling the locals with stories about the dangers of the canyons.

The Kolbs greatly enjoyed their stay in the bustling, friendly town. A local photographer let them use his darkroom, so they were able to develop their films and arrange to have them shipped back to their studio at the Grand Canyon. They replenished their supplies with local delicacies such as apples, melons and Vernal honey. The next day they saw Fagan off on the stage to Price, 120 miles distant, to catch a train back to his home in San Francisco, which he vowed never to leave again. The Kolbs were back on the river by 9 October.

They ended their journey at Needles, California on 8 January 1912. Ellsworth was not content to quit there, however; he went back in May 1913 and completed the remaining four hundred miles to the Gulf of California in just over a week. The brothers sold thousands of copies of their delightful book about their experiences on the river, and in addition, Ellsworth wrote an article for *National Geographic,* which appeared in the August 1914 issue.[35] Many visitors saw their film, which ran continuously in the studio until Ellsworth's death in 1976. Since Stone's book about his voyage was not published until 1932, *Through the Grand Canyon* was the first to reveal the beauties of the canyons to the public. Before the Kolbs' account was published in 1914, the Green was known only through the dramatic (and inaccurate) account of Major Powell, and through the legends that had been told and retold for generations about men going to their deaths on the river. The Kolbs' relatively easy passage of the canyons, as well as their writings and superb photographs, did much to put to rest some of the myths about the "impassable" Green.

The journeys of Julius Stone and the Kolb brothers were well recorded in film and in print, and that in itself was an important contribution to the human story of river travel. Viewed from a perspective of seventy years, however, the two journeys assume a far greater significance than simply a visual or verbal record. There are three important points to consider that set these two trips apart from all of those that had gone before.

First, boats. Their published accounts popularized the Galloway boat and introduced it to the infant sport of river running. To Galloway himself must go the credit for designing it, of course, but Stone and the Kolbs ensured that the idea would not die with him. The Galloway-style boat, with little variation from the basic design, remained the standard on the river for more than thirty years after Galloway's death in 1913. It was only supplanted by the inflatable raft, which was not available in large quantities until the end of World War II. Interestingly, many modern river runners, seeking a more challenging or purist way of running rapids, are returning to hard-hulled boats as their favored fast-water craft.

Second, technique. Again, it was Galloway who developed the stern-first method of running rapids, but it was the later voyagers who made it known to the general public. The Galloway method, as it is called, remains the standard to this day, whether in inflatable rafts or modern dories. Galloway's simple idea, made known to the world by the books and photographs of Julius Stone and the Kolb brothers, revolutionized fast-water navigation and indeed made it feasible.

Finally, and most important, motivation. Galloway loved the river and the canyons, but as we have seen, his real motivation was to reap the rich harvest of furs to be found there. In this he differed not at all from the other river runners since Ashley and his band of trappers in 1825. Manly had been seeking an easier way to the gold fields of California, Powell had been after scientific knowledge and the sure fame that a traverse of the river would bring; everyone wanted to get something out of the river.

Stone wanted to prove Major Powell wrong, and the Kolbs wanted photographs they could sell in their Grand Canyon studio. But even though these were their stated or implied reasons, there was something else behind their voyages. They were there for the adventure, for the thrill of doing something that few others had done. They were pleasure boaters, tourists. They were the vanguard of the many thousands of people, all over the world, who today run rivers for the challenge, the natural beauty, the solitude. Stone and the Kolbs represent a transition point in the history of the human use of the river, when people came not to exploit, but to experience. For the first time, men were beginning to approach the river on its own terms.

7

New Faces, New Ideas

By the time that Emery and Ellsworth Kolb went down the Green, the canyons were getting to be well known in some circles, and it was not uncommon to meet another river runner, instead of just ranchers, hermits, and outlaws.

As early as 1896, a man named George Flavell and his partner, Ramon Montos, set out from Green River, Wyoming, in the former's beautiful handmade boat.[1] Flavell had some experience with rowboats on the lower Colorado and knew what he was doing; he ran all of the rapids down to the Gates of Lodore without a hitch. After hearing and disregarding the usual stories about the river in Browns Park, he went on, a bit more cautiously, perhaps—he lined Winnie's Rapid, Disaster Falls, and Hell's Half Mile. He and Montos went all the way to the foot of the Grand Canyon, reaching Callville, Nevada, in October. About ten years later, a young lad from Jensen named Jens Jensen built his own boat and used it to run the Green from the Gates of Lodore, "just for fun." His friend Charlie Dennis, also of Jensen, was along for the trip, which they made in good shape.[2]

It was inevitable that sooner or later someone would try out a powered craft on the river. The first one to be built was in 1908, patriotically named the *Teddy R.* It was a small powered launch, which was used to make pleasure excursions up and down the river from Green

River, Wyoming. That same year saw a more ambitious, but ill-fated craft, the *Comet.* This was a stern wheeler, twelve feet wide and sixty feet long, which was financed and built at a cost of $25,000 by the Green River Navigation Company. The boat carried freight for the ranches and farms up and down the river. For a fare of five dollars, passengers could ride from Green River to Linwood, at the confluence of Henry's Fork, and back. As it turned out, however, the Green was too shallow most of the year for a boat of such magnificence, not to mention deep draft. After making only a couple of trips, it was tied up at the river-bank near Green River and abandoned. Finally, there was the *Sunbeam,* a gasoline-powered stern wheeler. From 1908 to 1910, it was also used for pleasure trips on the river, until it broke down near Big Piney, Wy-oming. The boat was hauled overland to Fremont Lake, modified, and used as a pleasure craft for many more years.[3]

In June of 1909, before Julius Stone began his Grand Traverse, two young men from St. Louis, Missouri, decided to try a boat trip on the Green as their spring vacation. Tom Martin and Jules B. Woodward were, according to the *Green River Star,* both "young men of rare abil-ity," members of the St. Louis Athletic Club, and excellent swimmers. Martin was an Annapolis graduate and a veteran of the Spanish-American War, the campaigns in the Philippines, and the Boxer Rebellion. Wood-ward was said to be a good swimmer and athlete. They set off on the spring rise in their specially designed boat, sure they were off on a grand adventure. The people of the town heard nothing more of them for a few days. The old-timers, used to such comings and goings, began to wag their heads wisely. Another pair of victims lost to the river, they all agreed.

Ten days later, however, the two came stumbling back to town, much worn and bedraggled. They had, it turned out, lost not only their boat, but their clothes and food as well, somewhere in Lodore. They were forced to walk about sixty miles over the sagebrush desert back to the railroad, where they hitched a ride to Green River. In an old cabin along the way they found an old pair of pants and tore them up to make coverings for their bleeding feet. Otherwise, they were naked as baby birds, and no doubt sunburned and scratched.[4] Although the Green must have seemed pretty tame around the Union Pacific rail-road bridge, it was still very much in command down in the canyons.

In one of the better districts of New York, young Web Todd was looking at a map of the West. He was a recent graduate of Princeton, and this hot summer of 1926 he was ready to take a vacation. No ordinary vacation, either, seeing the sights of Europe or lounging on the beaches of Coney Island. He wanted something different and exciting. As he studied his map, he realized that he had found just what he was looking for.[5]

Todd was looking at the Green River, and as he traced its course he noticed that it was crossed by rail lines at two different points: Green River, Wyoming, and Green River, Utah, a river distance of over three hundred miles. Here was the perfect vacation adventure, a trip by boat down the still largely unknown (at least in New York) Green River. The railroad connection made the trip look feasible. The first person Web thought of to accompany him on his grand adventure was F. Lemoyne Page, his roommate and best friend at Princeton. Page hadn't planned to take a vacation that year, but on hearing from his college chum, decided to go along.

Neither of the men knew anything about the Green River: Page commented that while he had heard of Green River Whiskey, he had certainly never heard of Green River, Wyoming. As the two friends studied the matter more carefully, they discovered that the trip was, as Page noted, "a real escapade, difficult, tedious, and hard." They also learned of some of the legends and stories about the river, all of which made them want to try it even more.

All plans were made, and they took the train for Green River on 23 July 1926. They had the good fortune to meet with Ellsworth Kolb in Pittsburgh, and that experienced river hand gave them some good advice and encouraged them to give it a try. A third friend from Princeton, "Og" West, met them in Chicago. On the morning of 26 July, the three roommates arrived in Green River. Todd had already arranged to buy two of the boats used by the U.S. Geological Survey in 1922 for three hundred dollars. After quite a bit of work putting the boats in shape, and hiring a guide, H. Elwyn Blake, who had been a boatman on the same survey, the Princeton crew was almost ready to go. The one thing they lacked were proper life jackets. They had not been able to find ready-made jackets anywhere. Blake, however, secured a supply of cork in town, so they resorted to frontier ingenuity and sewed their own.

Finally, on the morning of 4 August, all was ready. Curley Hale, the final member of the party, started the day by firing a rifle over their heads. After that rude awakening, they set off down the river. Since they had started below Flaming Gorge, they soon reached Carter Creek, just above Ashley Falls. They tried fishing in the clear stream, but without much luck. After a hike, lunch, and a swim in the little rapid at the mouth of the canyon, they moved on downstream and camped for the night.

The next day they passed the place where the U.S. Geological Survey had encountered Amos Hill, the Hermit of Red Canyon, but there was no sign of the old man. Perhaps the canyons were getting too crowded for him. Around noon, they came to Ashley Falls. Blake, who had been there before, noted that they inspected the rapid only briefly before running it; Page, on the other hand stated it was "after considerable study." Blake ran the first boat through; Page and Todd matched for the honor of rowing the other boat. Page won, and ran the boat through without trouble. To cap their successful passage of the rapid, all hands walked back upstream and swam through! Ashley Falls, the first of the fearsome rapids on the Green, was losing its bad reputation.

Later that afternoon, they came to a particularly difficult rapid that Blake had been warning them about all along—Red Creek. It looked as bad as they had feared, and as it was getting dark, they decided to line the boats through and then camp below. It is always a good feeling to be camped below a bad rapid, but in this case they were a bit too hasty. They began lining the first boat through the channel nearest the shore when their luck caught up with them. "Overconfidence proved to be their undoing," Blake noted sourly:

> Feeling that everything was proceeding in fine shape, I motioned for Curley to let the line out quickly. At the same instant a side current caught the boat . . . in a moment the cockpit had filled, the up-stream side of the boat sinking lower and lower until the boat was nearly submerged. . . . Our efforts [to move it] were in vain.[6]

They tried removing the hatch covers to lessen the pressure of the current. It didn't help any, but it did allow them to get to their soaked bedrolls and some food. After fixing a kettle of hot soup and drying their blankets around a huge fire, their spirits lifted and they turned in.

Blake was up early the next day to rig a windlass out of driftwood, while the others set to work moving boulders out of the channel to divert the force of the current away from the trapped boat. To their great joy, their combined efforts finally succeeded and the boat floated free. Except for some minor damage, it was none the worse for spending the night under water. The boat was soon repaired, and nosed through the new channel. A big storm was approaching when they reached Browns Park, just below the rapid, so they took refuge at the still-deserted Jarvie Ranch.

The party took its time floating through Browns Park, hunting for geese and stopping at ranches along the river. When they neared the end of the park, Todd, Page and West hired a car at the 2-Bar Ranch and made a trip to the Lodore Post Office to send off some letters and film. Blake stayed behind to get the boats ready for their big test, the ill-famed canyon of Lodore.

They passed Winnie's Rapid, which they called Loper Falls after Bert Loper, the head boatman on Blake's first trip four years before, without difficulty. Blake did break an oar, though, while Page, rowing the other boat, recorded that he ran it "safely, if not skillfully." They ran Upper Disaster Falls, with Todd at the oars of the second boat, and nosed both boats through the lower section. That night it rained, and they were glad for a tent made of a tarpaulin.

Triplet Falls had Blake worried. This long, twisting rapid is full of large rocks and tight turns, with disaster awaiting a wrong decision or a missed stroke of the oars. Although it doesn't have the reputation of Disaster Falls or Hell's Half Mile, it has proved the undoing of more than one boat.[7] Blake commented to Page that "perhaps he wouldn't need his bed roll that night so not to move it until he got through." Page wanted to run one of the boats through, but Blake felt that the college men, through very athletic, didn't have the skills necessary to negotiate the rapid, so he ran both boats through safely.

Hell's Half Mile was next, and it looked bad. Blake described it as a "raging demon." They carried some of their gear around the rapid, and Blake ran the first boat through. He got past the big boulder at the foot of the first drop in good shape, but snapped an oar in the rocks below and was soon high and dry on a rock in the middle of the channel. Here, he commented, he "had leisure to survey the situation." By standing in the water, he was able to work the boat free, but when he jumped back in to grab the oars, to his surprise the boat didn't budge.

After some confusing moments, he realized that the bowline was wedged firmly enough in the rocks to hold him in place:

> From this position I could view both the lower and upper portions of the rapid so I decided it might prove a point of vantage, from which I might view the running of the second boat, and perhaps be of assistance in case of accident. Accordingly, I motioned to Lem [Page] and succeeded in making him understand he was to bring the second boat through, while I waited in mid-stream. [8]

Page picks up the story:

> I was, of course, crazy to [run the boat]. . . . I ran quickly up, my heart "damn" near in my mouth, unloosened the tie rope, pushed off and here I was rushing into Hell's Half Mile [and] could see two big rocks just at the edge of the falls. Blake had said that it was absolutely imperative to go to the right of one of them. I had studied the falls from below and things looked entirely different from above, and I could not figure which was the rock. I believe I would have given everything I possessed to have been able to turn back, but there was no turning back then. I was by this time heading straight for the middle of the outer rock. To hit it I knew would be fatal. . . . I must go outside of it—if I could make it. I never pulled so hard for the life of the boat and perhaps my own depended on it [but] I saw that I could not miss [the rock] so hit it I did and despite all my pulling frantically on my port oar and was relieved to see the *Colorado,* after the first hit, slide nicely past the rock and head stern first downstream. . . . Then for a minute the boat and I were entirely submerged in the tremendous wave below. . . . As I shot through it my starboard oar lock came out. . . . In desperation I let go my port oar entirely and, although it seemed very long to me then, very quickly had the other lock in place. . . . I immediately straightened her out and followed the channel closest to the shore. . . . I grazed several [rocks] but none seriously. Then came a bad turn of the rapid but I got by it safely. I had passed Blake with his boat over on the side. . . . Full of exultation and relief I pulled over to a sandy beach. Hell's Half Mile was passed and I had come through it safely. [9]

It was a happy camp that night at Rippling Brook. All were in high spirits, and as Page exulted, "Why shouldn't we be? Everything bad was passed. . . . There wasn't a rapid below us that even had a name. We had had a remarkably successful trip. . . ." He spoke too soon, however. There were still five miles of Lodore to go, and the river was not yet through with them.

The next morning, Og West took the oars of the second boat to run the small rapid just below the camp. He had been warned that while easy, it had to be run carefully. Og was not up to the task, unfortunately; he froze at the oars and the boat crashed broadside onto one of the rocks in the rapid, quickly filling with water. Page was thrown out, losing his camera, and barely made it to shore. "We were all dumb-struck that a thing like this could happen now," Page wrote, "and we didn't know quite what to make of it."

They worked all that day trying to free the trapped boat, but this time even Blake's windlass was no help. The boat was too far from shore, the water too deep and swift. After breaking a couple of ropes trying to pull the boat free, they considered hiking out of the canyon to get a steel cable, but decided against it. Finally, reluctantly, they had to admit the boat and all in it was lost. Camp that night, with five of them in two bedrolls, was crowded and uneasy.

The next morning Todd tried to get out to the boat to reclaim some of their gear, but he was unable to even reach the boat. "The high confining walls which had seemed so beautiful and grand a day or so before now almost drove me mad," Page recorded. "This disaster had been so unexpected, so unnecessary, so ridiculous." Page had suffered the most in the accident; besides his camera, he had lost all of his exposed film.[10]

There was nothing left to do at that point but load up the remaining boat and go. Five passengers were too much for the one boat, so they walked around the rest of the rapids, while Blake rowed the boat through. They passed Echo Park and Whirlpool Canyon that day and stopped for the night at the Ruple Ranch in Island Park. Blake guided the boat through the rapids of Split Mountain Canyon by himself, but in the calm stretches, the men doubled up at the oars to make better time. The river had lost its attraction.

When they reached Jensen, Page and Og West decided that since it was entirely too crowded in one boat and their vacations were almost over anyway they would leave the river here. For them, the accident had ruined the rest of the trip. Blake, Curley, and Web Todd continued on down to Green River, Utah, which they reached on 19 August.

For the boys from Princeton, their trip down the Green was no more than an especially exciting summer vacation. Its importance in the history of river running lies mostly in the attitudes displayed and the assurance with which they started out on the journey. What was a

dangerous expedition into the unknown less than a century before was
now becoming something done by college boys on a lark.

There were others, however, who would not have shared that opinion. Scarcely two years later a party sponsored by the *Denver Post* set
out from Lily Park to "explore" the canyon of the Yampa.[11] The head-
line splashed across the front page was attention-grabbing: EXPEDITION
TO RISK DEATH IN WILD REGION, it declared in bold type. The lead article, published in late August of 1928, went on to claim that "no man
has ever traveled" down the Yampa, "which remains completely un-
explored." Never mind that Galloway and his ten-year-old son had
floated the river twenty years before, and Major Powell and his crew
had rowed up the river forty years before that. This was the era of yellow journalism, and the *Denver Post,* a Hearst paper, knew that the
more lurid the headlines, the better the issue would sell.

The expedition consisted of A. G. Birch, Fred Dunham, Charles
Mace, and Bert Moritz, Jr. They started on 21 August in two boats,
the *Leakin' Lena* and the *Prickly Heat.* They had hardly gotten into the
canyon before one of the boats crashed on a rock, as observers watched
from the canyon rim. The trip had started badly, and it soon got worse.
On the twenty-fourth, the *Lena* was pinned against a rock and lost, and
with it most of their film, food, and all of their camping gear. While
the other three struggled to get the remaining boat down the rocky channel, Birch, who had hurt his back, went for help. After walking down
the canyon for three days, he was finally able to climb out of a draw
and walk twelve miles across the sagebrush to a ranch. As he reached
the ranch, he met a rescue party just starting out to find the river explorers. The rest of the world, of course, knew nothing of their misad-
ventures, and when the men failed to show up at a rendezvous, their
editor feared the worst.

For all their hardships, however, Birch could not fail to be impressed
with the beauty of the canyon. He filed the following breathless dispatch before returning to the canyon with the rescue party:

> Can't describe wild beauty, gorgeousness and majesty of this canon. It
> is really nine or ten Zion canyons placed on end. With all Zion's wild
> colors and far more ruggedness. Deserves to be a National Park or Na-
> tional Monument along with Zion, Yosemite and all others. It would give
> thrill of their lives to easterners. . . .[12]

Birch concluded the dispatch on a brave note: "Don't worry about us. We'll make it."

Make it they did, although they still might have had doubts. The Yampa at low water is a very difficult river to navigate, the channel rocky and narrow, the river full of small, tricky rapids. Pushing and paddling a heavy, clumsy wooden boat would have required enormous exertion. "None of us ever expected to get back alive," Birch declared in a story filed the day they started back for Denver. One cannot help but wonder how much of the danger was exaggerated for the benefit of the readers—after all, a safe, easy river journey would not have sold many papers. At any rate, the Yampa was now officially explored.

The fifty-mile journey had taken the four men two weeks to complete. By the time they reached Castle Park, the remaining boat was so battered that they abandoned it on the side of the river. Still, all felt it worth the trip and were lavish in their praise of the beauties of the region. The story was picked up by leading daily newspapers all over the country and received wide circulation. The expedition, for all its talk of hardship and disaster, proved in the end to be one more hole in the shroud of myth surrounding the canyons.

The 1930s were the turning point in the story of human use of the river. All the threads of the past and future of river running came together in that pivotal decade. Boat design, the type of trips, the people who ran the river all began to undergo a change. The midthirties also saw the advent of commercial river running, and by 1940 there was more than one outfit "piloting dudes" down the river.

Just five years after the *Post* party, in the fall of 1932, a Salt Lake City furrier named Fred Launer bought a Berger foldboat.[13] The old-timers at Green River must have snickered when they saw the collapsible canvas and wood craft laid out on the riverbank. Anyone knew that a man needed a good sturdy wooden boat, not one of these flimsy French contraptions, to face the canyons. Nonetheless, Launer and his companion, Dr. Charles Plummer, were confident that the maneuverable kayak could safely navigate the rapids. Launer had a little more confidence than Dr. Plummer, it would seem, for the latter walked around all the rapids taking pictures, while Fred ran the boat through. Except for a few easily repaired punctures in the fabric hull of the boat, they completed their trip without mishap.

In 1936 Anton R. Backus of Salt Lake City decided he would give the river a try and started out from the Gates of Lodore in a "scow-type, partially decked punt.''[14] The waves crashing around the big rock in Winnie's Rapid, however, were enough to convince him that perhaps running the river was not such a good idea, and he pulled the *Illinois Girl* up on the talus at the foot of the rapid and left her right there. As recently as 1982, the weathered hulk could still be seen, a testament to the power that Lodore can hold over men's imaginations.

Imagination can work both ways, however. Toward the end of the pivotal decade of the thirties, more and more men, and even a few women, began to respond to the call of the river and the rapids.

In the fall of 1937, Haldane Holmstrom, better known as Buzz, went into the forest around his native Coquille, Oregon, looking for just the right cedar tree.[15] He found it, and out of it built a beautiful sixteen-foot, Galloway-style boat. He wanted to float the Green and the Colorado right down to the newly completed Hoover Dam. A friend was supposed to accompany him, but backed out at the last minute, so Buzz decided to go it alone. Except for the shadowy Denis Julien, Holmstrom is the first known person to do so. To get an idea of what lay ahead of him, he looked up that old man of the river, Bert Loper. Bert assured him that the river was passable, no matter what the ''wise men'' of Green River might say.

Buzz started from Green River on 4 October, a cloudy, threatening day. For the first few days, floating through the monotonous clay hills down to Flaming Gorge, he was nervous and edgy, anxious to get to the rapids of Red Canyon. His boat drew more water than he had expected, causing it to hang up on the many sandbars in the river. He worried that the low water level would also mean that the rapids would be full of exposed rocks.

On the eighth he reached Ashley Falls and to his relief ran it without any problems. Just below the rapid, at a ford across the river, he ran into a group of men returning from driving a herd of cows to Green River from Vernal and stopped to talk with them. The next day he came to Red Creek Rapid, which Buzz recorded was ''a dirty son of a gun to put it mild—steep, long, and rocky.'' Figuring that he wanted to see how far down the river he could get and not how many rapids he could run, Buzz reluctantly unloaded his equipment and ran the boat through empty. Three loads of gear carried over a quarter of a mile were enough for him: ''If there are any more long portages, about half my stuff is going overboard.''[16]

Browns Park seemed to be completely deserted, so he had only the beaver, deer, and birds for company. The Depression and falling beef prices had ruined most of the small ranchers in the park. The only person he encountered, in fact, was a man named Longdon who ran a tourist camp at the Gates of Lodore. The owner, John Grounds, took tourists in a motorboat two miles into the canyon, where he had built a small cabin. The operation continued into the 1940s, and the cabin can still be seen today.[17] After visiting with Longdon, the last person he would see for some time, Buzz headed into Lodore.

He made it through the first series of rapids. Stopping at Winnie's Rapid to scout, he noticed Tony Backus's boat abandoned below. Undaunted by this reminder, Buzz continued on downriver to the first major obstacle, Disaster Falls. The upper part presented no serious problem, but to get through Lower Disaster, he portaged his gear and lined the empty boat past the undercut cliff. He had to do the same thing in the lower end of Triplet Falls, and at the foot of that rapid he found more reminders of previous attempts to navigate the canyon: "There is a stern metal . . . tank with hatch cover, out of a river boat, pulled up on the bank here, also a pair of oars, one broken."[18] Camp that night was plagued by a huge fire he inadvertently set when his small cook fire spread to a pile of driftwood. He was showered with ashes and embers and forced to move several times during the night.

Buzz was lucky, it would seem, in running Hell's Half Mile. Despite bouncing off a few rocks, getting some water in his boat, and losing an oarlock at a critical moment, he made it through with boat and self intact and right side up. A leak in the boat had him worried, but it turned out to be nothing more than a screwhole with no screw in it.

He floated the next day on past Echo Park and down to Jones Hole. Whirlpool Canyon was full of rocks, but still presented no serious problems. Even the rocky channel didn't stop him from admiring the scenery and enjoying the animals that visited him in his camp. Stopping at the Ruple Ranch the next day for dinner, he learned that Art Ruple had died the year before, but his brother, who now ran the place, knew many of the old-time river runners, such as Than Galloway, Julius Stone and the Kolb brothers.

Split Mountain Canyon at low water is shallow and tricky, but after Lodore, Buzz breezed through. Camped a couple of miles above the mouth, he witnessed a violent thunderstorm:

I wouldn't have missed this for anything. There are creeks falling over the cliffs all around, and right across the river is almost a landslide: a big strong stream bringing down rocks by the ton, the river is dark red, almost black. . . .[19]

He made it to Jensen the next day, and after getting a hotel room, hitched a ride into Vernal. That proved to be one of the more difficult tasks of the entire trip; two weeks on the river and he looked like just another bum. He needed supplies and equipment for himself and his boat, but most of all he wanted to meet some other men who were beginning to be well known in the small world of river runners: Frank Swain, Bus Hatch, and Royce "Cap" Mowry, all residents of Vernal. They had gone through the Grand Canyon in 1934, and Buzz was anxious to get some advice about the river he was to face later on. Unfortunately, they were all out of town and Buzz missed them.

After spending only a day or so in Vernal, Buzz shoved off into the flat water of the Uinta Basin, heading downstream for Desolation Canyon, the Grand Canyon, and Hoover Dam. When he reached Lake Mead on 20 November 1937, he refused a tow across the still water, preferring to row his boat until the bow touched the back of Hoover Dam. Having soloed all the way from Wyoming, he wasn't about to accept any help.

The next year, Buzz was back for another run, this time in the company of Amos Burg, a free-lance photographer and experienced river runner who had already been down the Snake, the Columbia, the Yellowstone, and other rivers. At Burg's suggestion, Buzz planned to go on to the San Francisco Exposition after the trip to exhibit his boat and give illustrated lectures about the river. An article in the *Saturday Evening Post* about his solo run had made him a celebrity. Burg planned to film the trip, sell the film rights, and sell the story to *National Geographic*.

By this time, however, it was no longer possible to make a solo run down the Green and not meet anyone else. In 1938, in fact, the river must have seemed downright crowded. So many people were getting on the river that for a period in the late summer and early fall of that year not a single issue of the weekly *Vernal Express* went by without at least one front-page story on river running. In November, there were four separate parties on the river at one time. No wonder the hermits were moving out.

When Holmstrom and Amos Burg started their trip, Buzz was back in his homemade boat, but Burg was rowing something new on the river: an inflatable rubber raft. It had been custom made to his specifications by the B. F. Goodrich Company. Amos and Buzz wanted to do the entire river, starting from its source in the Wind River Mountains, and so they launched just below Green River Lakes. The channel was too rocky, however, and the river too low, and they ended up making a portage by truck to Green River. There they got their gear into shape for the canyons below and added a passenger, artist and cartographer Phil Lundstrom. They got back on the river on 3 September.

Burg was exultant to be on the river, praising even the badlands below Green River as romantic and colorful. They made good time, undeterred by the rapids in Red Canyon. They ran Ashley Falls and Red Creek Rapid, the bane of so many early river travelers, with hardly a second thought. The end of their first week on the river found them in Lodore. First Upper and Lower Disaster Falls, and then Triplet Falls were put behind them. Burg hung the *Charlie* on a rock in Triplet, but that was the only trouble to speak of. At Hell's Half Mile they portaged their gear partway, and on further consideration, Burg's boat as well. Buzz ran his through the rapid.

After the customary stop at the Ruple Ranch, they headed on down through Split Mountain and reached Jensen on the fourteenth. The riverbank from the mouth of the canyon to Jensen was lined with delegations from Vernal welcoming the river runners. They were taken to the Vernal Lion's Club and treated, or subjected, to a lavish dinner, speeches, and other festivities.

A couple of days of this treatment was enough for both of them. Lundstrom left as planned, and Burg and Holmstrom were more than glad to get back to "the river silences, the caress of the blowing breezes, and to watch again the drifting stars."

While Buzz and Amos Burg were receiving the accolades of the Vernal Lion's Club, another river party was quietly getting ready to launch at the end of a bad road about three miles from Green River, Wyoming. No one even knew of their plans until a local reporter got wind of them. This was a rather unusual group, even among the individualists that had been down the river so far. For one thing, they

Bernard and Genevieve DeColmont at Green River, September 1938.

had come all the way from France just to run the Green River. For another, one of them was a woman.[20]

The French travelers were Bernard DeColmont, his young bride Genevieve, and Antoine DeSeyne, all three seasoned kayakers. They had run many rivers in Europe and had just completed a journey down the Nile. Now they were in southwestern Wyoming, their stated object, as they told a reporter from the *Green River Star,* in coming so far was to try "the technique they use in running waters in Europe, and with which they are familiar, with the most wonderful river in the world." Their boats were fifteen-foot folding kayaks, with a rubberized canvas hull stretched over a wooden frame. The Frenchmen had the utmost confidence in their small craft and European technique, going so far as to declare that they felt them "to be safer than boats heretofore used on the river." At the same time, they had "no illusions as to the danger before them," having studied "all the books and magazine articles covering previous expeditions." To minimize the dangers, the French adventurers wore protective helmets when running rapids, each boat was equipped with a cover to keep the waves out, and there was one final item of safety gear: "Genevieve DeColmont . . . carries a stuffed toy giraff[e] beside her in the boat. [Bernard] prefers a stuffed Teddy bear and Mr. DeSeyne chooses a little toy pig.''[21]

Their camp equipment was also much more modern than that of contemporary American river runners. They carried down sleeping bags and air mattresses instead of bedrolls, a Primus gas stove to cook with, and rubber waterproof bags. Like many river runners today, their main load seemed to be canned beer, although it was for hygiene, not pleasure. ''They seemed to fear bad drinking water more than bad running water,'' as Dock Marston put it.[22]

The French trio took their time getting down the river. They were overtaken at Red Creek Rapid by a group from the Utah Fish and Game Department, who had left Hideout Flat below Flaming Gorge six days after them.[23] The fish and game party—consisting of Lee Kay, Earl Clyde, Roy DeSpain, Dr. D. I. Rasmussen, and Wes Eddington—was conducting a survey of the wildlife in the river canyon. Their boats were of the proven Galloway design, made by Roy DeSpain, a vocational arts teacher from Springville, Utah, to Bus Hatch's specifications. Lee Kay, the leader of the party, declared them to be ''the best ever to be taken through the canyons.''

The two parties stayed fairly close to each other as they went down the river. At Hell's Half Mile, they camped together and since it was Genevieve's twenty-second birthday, the Americans cooked a special dinner in her honor.[24]

The survey party reached Jensen first and reported on the progress of the Europeans. Amazingly, the kayakers actually seemed to enjoy running rapids:

> When Bernard DeColmont and Antoine DeSeyne run the fast rapids their entire countenances radiate a delight never before shown by rivermen. . . . Genevieve DeColmont, wife of Mr. Colmont, is enjoying every minute of the trip and is almost overcome with enthusiasm when attempting to describe the unusual scenery. . . . The two men take the lead in traveling down the canyon rapids, with the young bride traveling a little slower, following behind. At times when Mr. DeColmont and his companion pass from sight around a sharp bend in the river, Genevieve will scream out ''Bernard, is this our river's end?'' inferring that their happy honeymoon had ended abruptly and tragically. Genevieve and Bernard were married August 1 in Paris.[25]

The French river runners reached Jensen the first week of October. Since they were in no hurry, they stopped over for four days to enjoy the hospitality of the town and stayed with local riverman Bus Hatch and his family.

There are almost one hundred miles of flat water between Jensen and the head of Desolation Canyon. The French adventurers borrowed an outboard motor from Wes Eddington[26] and rigged it to a frame lashed between two of the boats. They towed DeSeyne and his boat until they reached Desolation Canyon. They made it all the way to Lee's Ferry at the end of Glen Canyon, and had planned to continue on through the Grand Canyon, but ice in the river made them change their minds. When the DeColmonts returned to France, they published a small book of their photographs, *Trois Francais en kayak sur le Green River et le Colorado.* Knowledge of the Green was beginning to cross state and even national boundaries; it was becoming an international river, no longer the exclusive preserve of Utah river runners.

Meanwhile, at Henry's Fork, a young man from Salt Lake City named Stewart Gardiner assembled his German foldboat, ordered from a catalog, and pushed away from the shore.[27] No articles in the paper, no photographers, no delegations of townspeople—just him, his boat, and the river. Gardiner was representative of a new generation of river runners in more ways than one. Besides the fact that he started his trip without fanfare, he was planning to go only from Henry's Fork to Jensen, about a week's journey. Before him, almost all the river parties had been full-fledged expeditions, the usual goal being to run the entire 1,800 miles from Wyoming to Mexico. Gardiner was not on an expedition—he was on a river trip.

He started on Sunday 23 October and by noon Monday had already passed Ashley Falls, which gave him no trouble. He lined Red Creek Rapid; it was too shallow and rocky to run. Just below Red Creek he lost his spare paddle somehow, which was to cause him trouble later. Lodore slowed him down; he lined Winnie's Rapid and Upper Disaster Falls, tearing a hole in his boat in the process. He tore another hole in the hull while running the lower part of the rapid. "There are so many rocks in the river," Gardiner wrote in "A Trip Down the Green River," "that the water boils around them, rather than run a straight channel as in Red Canyon." He made it through the rest of Lodore, only to run his boat up on a half-submerged rock and capsize in Whirlpool Canyon. He lost his paddle in this mishap and came close to drowning when he discovered, to his dismay, that his life jacket was defective and wouldn't keep him afloat. Fortunately the boat caught on a rock downstream, and Gardiner was spared the long walk out to Vernal. He carved a new paddle out of driftwood and made his way out of the canyons without further trouble. After spending a couple of days hunting for deer and arrowheads near Jensen, he packed up his boat, caught a bus, and went home.

The next year, Gardiner was back, along with a companion named Alexander Grant, for another foldboat run of the Green, which they eventually wrote up and had published in a book called *Fabulous Foldboat Holidays.* Grant went on to run many other rivers in his foldboat, the *Escalante,* including a run of the Grand Canyon in 1941.

In 1939 Charles F. Mann of Pennsylvania decided to test his skills in a ten-year-old, fourteen-foot folding kayak.[28] The rocks in Lodore tore numerous holes in his boat, and at one point he was sucked under a ledge by the strong current and almost drowned. He lost his camera, gun, part of his food, and worst of all, his pipes, though he saved his tobacco. It was soaked, so he had to dry it out in a frying pan and roll his own cigarettes. Despite all the mishaps, he was still able to get his boat all the way to Lee's Ferry.

The first decades of the twentieth century were pivotal ones in the history of river running. While still mostly local people were on the river, a change was beginning by the end of the 1930s. River running was no longer exclusively a man's pursuit, either. Just a couple of months before Genevieve DeColmont piloted her foldboat down the Green, two women became the first commercial passengers to float the lower Green. Dr. Elzada Clover and her assistant, Lois Jotter, two botanists from the University of Minnesota, started from Green River, Utah, in July on a commercial trip led by Norm Nevills of Mexican Hat, Utah.

In September of 1939, while Charles Mann was struggling through Lodore, German tanks were rolling across the Polish countryside. By the time Mann reached Lee's Ferry, the conquest was complete, and Europe was at war. Nothing much happened, either on the Green River or in Europe, during that uneasy winter of 1939–40. On 10 May though, German forces smashed into Holland, Belgium, and France. It was inevitable that even the United States would be drawn into the ever-widening conflict. American involvement in World War II had repercussions that would reach as far as the remote canyons of the Green

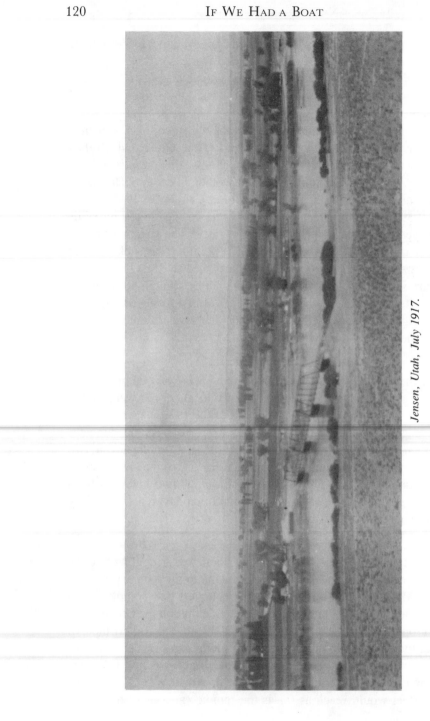

Jensen, Utah, July 1917.

and the Yampa, and affected the rivers in ways that no one could have imagined.

Meanwhile, on 9 May, the *Vernal Express* reported that engineers and workmen had begun the exploratory core drilling for a dam at Echo Park. The dam had been on the drawing boards for many years, and the residents of the Uinta Basin looked expectantly to the benefits its completion would bring. There were others, however, who were not so pleased at the prospect. A battle of an entirely different sort was shaping up over the activities of the busy engineers at the mouth of Whirlpool Canyon.

Surveyors and Dam Builders

Adventurers, outfitters, and explorers were not the only ones concerned with the Green River. Powell's surveys had only been an early indication of an interest that the federal government has maintained in the river. The engineers and administrators of the newly organized U.S. Reclamation Service were now determined to see those ideas realized. What better place for water storage projects than the upper basin of the Green, with all of that water going to waste, with deep canyons just made for reservoirs, with thousands and thousands of acres of fertile land wanting only water to make it "blossom as the rose," and with a population of industrious and thrifty Mormon farmers awaiting just such an opportunity?

Another aspect of the river basin that the engineers had their eyes on was the generation of electricity by hydropower—simple, clean, and relatively inexpensive. Again, the area around the Green seemed the perfect choice: a growing population; cities, farms, mines that could benefit from a source of cheap power; and, in many ways most important, vast mineral wealth underlying the entire region. Coal, iron ore, copper, oil, oil shale, gilsonite, uranium, and potash were but a few of the minerals awaiting exploitation. The cost involved in mining, processing, and shipping ore and minerals had always been the prohibitive factor blocking the full development of these resources. A ready

supply of electrical power could change all that, bring light, civilization, industry, and prosperity to the traditionally economically depressed
areas of eastern Utah, western Colorado, and southern Wyoming. City
fathers, land speculators, and engineers were as excited as the residents.

A new force began to intrude in the middle of plans and specula-
tions, however. "Butterfly-chasers," as they were derisively called,
looked at the canyons and the rivers and saw something there that the
engineers had already factored out of their calculations. Conservationists
didn't see kilowatts or acre-feet, but solitude, adventure, and the marvelous handiwork of nature in the canyons and valleys. These groups
of men and women were part of a movement to preserve the last remaining areas of natural beauty in a region already heavily taxed by
the demands of industry and agriculture.

The conservation movement had gotten its start during the 1870s
and gained momentum under Theodore Roosevelt, during the era of
reform, trust-busting, and progressive social movements. Tensions between those who would develop the West's resources for the best use
of the country and its people, and those who would preserve parts of
it for future generations, simmered until just after World War II, and
indeed continue to this day. In the 1940s and 1950s, Echo Park became the stage and focus for one of the most bitterly fought conservation battles of the century. Decisions made as a result of the debate set
precedent for later clashes.

How did all this come about? The plans for the Echo Park Dam
were the result of years of planning and study by dedicated, thorough
professionals. That anyone would object to their plans was a source
first of surprise, then resentment and bitterness. Before looking at the
Echo Park Dam and the controversy it engendered, one must first go
back and trace the development of the concept of the Colorado River
Storage Project.

The search for practical uses for the canyons had been going on
since the turn of the century. In 1901 an intrepid resident of Jensen
named Harry Ratliff had walked the canyons from Echo Park to the
mouth of Split Mountain Canyon trying to determine the suitability of
the canyon for a railroad bed.[1] In the fall of 1909, Julius Stone encountered some engineers from the Reclamation Service when he passed
the Gates of Lodore. The engineers had been there since 1907, drilling

core holes to test the suitability of the bedrock as a damsite for a massive structure that would turn all of Browns Park into a lake.[2] Surprisingly, the drilling crew failed to find bedrock upon which to anchor the foundations of a dam, and the project was abandoned.[3] There may have been other reasons, however: "the work has been hampered by high water and by the difficulty, on account of the remoteness of the site, of getting men to carry on the work."[4]

The search for damsites went on, however, undeterred by either high water or remoteness. In 1914 a survey party from the U.S. Geological Survey, led by Eugene Clyde LaRue, floated through Flaming Gorge and Horseshoe canyons to Hideout Flat, taking note of potential damsites along the way.[5] The Utah Power and Light Company sent a survey party of their own down the river in 1917 to study streamflow and damsites. The utility crew had seventeen-foot boats "specially designed for Green River navigation; the bow and stern about the same height." They found good damsites at Flaming Gorge, the Gates of Lodore, and Split Mountain on the upper river.[6]

All of these surveys were of short river stretches, however, and so were limited in their usefulness. What was needed was a complete and comprehensive topographic map and profile of the canyons, "properly correlating the several isolated surveys of reservoir sites. . . ." Ralf R. Woolley, a hydraulic engineer, set about putting together just such a survey in the early months of 1922.[7]

Woolley was a thorough and practical man, an engineer's engineer. For the survey, he had three boats built in California. Two of these were Galloway-style boats, although a bit longer at eighteen feet than those built by Nathaniel. The other was sixteen feet long and "similar in plan to a common rowboat."[8] All were decked fore and aft, with sturdy hatch covers fastened by wing nuts. The frames were oak, and to protect against abrasion during portages and linings, there were oak strips fastened along the sides of the hull. On the water, passengers sat on the hatches, while the oarsmen rowed the boat from the central cockpit.

In choosing a guide and head boatman, Woolley was no less thorough. He selected Bert Loper, a man whose reputation on the river was second only to Galloway's. Loper was quite well known among rivermen on the Colorado for his traverses of Cataract and Glen canyons, the latter upstream at least once. The other boatmen, who were also to serve as rodmen for the survey, were L. B. Lunt and H. E. Blake.

Two other engineers, including one from Utah Power and Light Co., and a cook completed the party. The naming of the boats was thought best left up to the boatmen, and after some deliberation they were named after the three states they would pass through: *Utah, Wyoming,* and *Colorado.*

The survey got on the river on 13 July 1922 after an evening spent at a dinner given in honor of the party by the Community Club of Green River. The night's entertainment, Woolley recorded, included the customary telling of "vivid tales of unsuccessful attempts to navigate the canyons by daring adventurers."

On the river, Woolley found the sixty miles of meanders above Flaming Gorge through "barren wasteland . . . somewhat monotonous." He recorded that many of the ranches along the river were now abandoned, the once hopeful owners having given up a losing battle with alkalai soil, deep snow, and baking sun.

The actual surveying got started about a mile above Henry's Fork, to tie in with the survey of 1914. Woolley wrote that "the river appears to drop into a hole, in the Uinta Range, and this is no doubt the 'suck' spoken of by Beckwourth." The party passed through Flaming Gorge, Horseshoe, and Kingfisher canyons in quick succession. The ever-observant engineer noted that in Kingfisher Canyon there were still plenty of the birds that had given it its name.

The boatmen began to earn their pay in Red Canyon. In the first five miles they ran nine rapids, including one more than a half-mile long. Below Carter Creek, one of the boats became firmly lodged on a submerged rock and all efforts by the boatman to dislodge it were in vain. Woolley described the unconventional method used to free the boat:

> Fortunately the *Utah* was still above the rapid and went to the rescue. The current was swift, and for a few minutes it looked as if the *Utah* would shoot by without getting near enough to give any assistance. Finally, in his effort to get closer, the boatman turned against the current, and the *Utah* bumped the *Wyoming,* knocking her free and solving what might otherwise have been a difficult problem.[9]

Just downstream, where Trail and Allen creeks entered the river, the survey party encountered Amos Hill, a seventy-one-year-old hermit who said he had lived in that spot for twenty years. He had a small garden, a few cows, some corn and alfalfa planted. When he needed other supplies—two or three times a year—he packed them in from Linwood, twenty miles away, or Vernal, forty-five miles across the mountains. His home, "or hovel was a crude tepee of boards over a small hole in the ground [which] might be classed as a good sized dog kennel."

Hill claimed, furthermore, to have floated the canyons of the Green on a raft with his horse along. This raised the eyebrows of the skeptical surveyors: "one who has been through the canyons would be justified in believing [it] impossible."[10]

Soon after leaving the hermit, the surveyors reached Ashley Falls. This obstacle the boatmen ran without trouble, although not without scouting the rapid thoroughly. Just below the falls they stopped to make a survey of a potential damsite near Cart Creek, the future site of Flaming Gorge Dam.

The last major obstruction on this stretch of river was Red Creek Rapid. Thanks to a timely warning from a rancher who lived above it, they were able to make a safe passage. After two peaceful days floating through Browns Park, they came to the Gates of Lodore, "and as the boats glided through . . . that same feeling of gloom which Ashley noticed on the countenances of his men was experienced by every man in the party." Nor was their foreboding misplaced; in Winnie's Rapid, the *Utah* crashed into a boulder in the middle of the channel, which knocked a hole in the stern. This took only about an hour to repair, but it must have seemed a very inauspicious beginning for their passage of Lodore. Upper Disaster Falls gave them no trouble, but the lower part looked too dangerous to try at the low water level. Camp was made at the head of the rapid, and around that night's campfire, Woolley noted, "opinions were not wanting as to the best way to get the boats through."

The next morning, they nosed the boats through the worst part of the rapid. This involved standing in water just deep enough to float the boats and slowly moving them past the rapid. This labor, and portaging all their gear and supplies around the falls early in the morning, "was a great stimulant to the appetites, and no one needed a second invitation to breakfast."[11]

Triplet Falls gave them no trouble, but one look at Hell's Half Mile convinced the boatmen that in the low water of late July, a portage would be necessary if they wanted to avoid damage to their boats. After giving it some "careful study," however, the boatmen decided that the boats, if emptied, could be run through after all. The crews portaged their equipment and provisions—Woolley, ever the careful engineer,

Aerial view of Echo Park. Steamboat Rock is in the center, the Yampa River is on the upper left, and the Green River is on the lower left (the Echo Park Dam would have been built at the head of Whirlpool Canyon, just out of the picture in the lower right corner).

noted that it took forty-three loads of sixty to seventy pounds each, carried almost half a mile to get past the rapid[12]—and the boats were run through with only a few knocks and scrapes. The men were exhausted from their exertions, but some clean clothes and a dip in the river were enough to put them back in good spirits and give everyone a good appetite.

Hell's Half Mile was the last major obstacle for the survey team. Whirlpool and Split Mountain canyons were hardly worth mentioning in the log, except to note that the latter was a "decidedly thrilling ride." Along the way, they surveyed two more potential damsites, one of them just around the corner from Echo Park in the mouth of Whirlpool Canyon. This site would assume far greater importance than Woolley and his crew could ever have imagined.

The 1922 U.S. Geological Survey's survey ended at Green River, Utah, in August. They had been very successful, having finished and published the first complete and accurate topographic map of the Green from Green River, Wyoming to Green River, Utah, and having mapped and surveyed fourteen potential damsites.

Now that the engineers had reduced the river to numbers and lines on graphs, it was up to the politicians and bureaucrats to take the figures and turn them into something else, a plan that went beyond even Powell's land-reclamation plans. The then unheard-of concept of multiple use—hydroelectric power generation, water storage, and recreation—would change the face of the river forever.

The year was 1946. American was ready to take the great national energies that had been developed to bring about the defeat of the Axis in World War II and turn them to more peaceful goals. One of these was harnessing the West's greatest natural resource, the Colorado River. During and immediately following the war, survey parties from the U.S. Geological Survey had once again been sent down the river, to collect the data needed to complete the plans for the project. Back in Washington, D.C., the Bureau of Reclamation was putting before Congress the most massive reclamation project ever conceived, the Colorado River Storage Project. This ambitious plan called for the construction of five major storage and hydroelectric units on the Colorado and its tributaries. It would encompass six states and include a dozen lesser projects connected with the main units. These combined projects would store forty million acre-feet of water, which would irrigate almost 400,000 acres, and produce 1,650,000 kilowatts.[13]

One of the proposed units in the plan, and one that supporters called the centerpiece of the whole idea, was the Echo Park Dam. This seven-hundred-foot concrete arch dam, located about a mile downstream from Echo Park, would, along with its smaller subsidiary in Split Mountain Canyon, flood Lodore, the Yampa Canyon, Browns Park, Island Park, and most of Whirlpool Canyon. Almost all of the proposed reservoir was within the boundaries of Dinosaur National Monument. The Monument itself had originally been only fifteen acres set aside to protect the Jurassic deposits of dinosaur bones about ten miles above Jensen, Utah. In 1938, however, it had been expanded by presidential decree to more than two hundred thousand acres, to protect the scenic values of the very canyons that the dam builders now proposed to flood. This proposal, to build a major reclamation project in an area supposedly protected within the national park system, caused a controversy that started slowly, but soon built to such a fever pitch that the feelings it generated have still not subsided.

One of the reasons that the controversy caused such strong emotion was that the residents of eastern Utah, western Colorado, and southern Wyoming placed such high hopes on the dam and the economic boost its construction would surely bring. This "three-corner" region was "painfully self-conscious of its unfulfilled potential."[14] Businessmen, ranchers, and farmers were starting to feel the pinch caused by the shutdown of defense industries at the end of the war. The construction of the two dams and accompanying power plants, roads, and transmission lines would take years, and employ thousands of workmen, who would in turn live, eat, and spend their wages in the small towns encompassed by the three-state area.

Besides the economic boost from construction, the dams would provide power and water that would, in the vision of its supporters, transform the Intermountain West. "Power from Echo Park will permit large tonnage production of phosphorus and make possible the reclamation of many thousands of acres of fertile lands along Green River," predicted engineer and part-time Jensen resident Harry Ratliff.[15] A pamphlet put out by the Republican party of Utah declared:

> The project will provide the necessary water to turn arid but fertile desert land into drought-free, food-producing acreage [and] conserve the precious, limited water supplies of the mountain west and end the present colossal erosion and water loss.[16]

Another pamphlet touched on a note that was especially sensitive to all Americans at the dawn of the Cold War—national defense:

> Under the threat of atomic warfare, industries are scattering to the sparsely populated areas of the West. These industries need power in amounts that can come only from large-scale power dams. . . .[17]

Finally, there was recreation. Proponents of the dam pointed out that "the only . . . access [to Echo Park] is down the wild, turbulent rapids of these rivers, reputed to be among the most hazardous in the world by the handful of adventurous river runners who have participated in this dangerous sport."[18] Another brochure declared:

> Dinosaur National Monument is now a no-man's land because of its inaccessibility. Today only a few hundred adventuresome souls dare risk their necks to ride the rapids of the Yampa and Green Rivers through otherwise impenetrable canyons.[19]

Pro-dam pamphlet from about 1950.

The dam would change all of that. The "safe, still waters" of the reservoir would transform "no-man's land" into a national pleasuring ground that would "entertain in comfort and with safety hundreds of thousands of pleasure seekers from every section of the nation."[20] To accommodate the expected multitude of vacationers, plans called for the construction of boat harbors, swimming beaches, cabins, lodges, two thousand picnic sites, four thousand camping spaces, two hundred miles of foot and bridle paths, one main museum near the site of the dam, and "seven strategically located secondary or wayside museums."[21]

Furthermore, the Aqualantes, or "water-vigilantes," claimed, the dam would not change the canyons that much. The reservoir would only cover the rocky talus at the bottom of the canyons, leaving the sculptured walls untouched. Indeed, an artist's conception of the entire reservoir area in a brochure published by the Upper Colorado Grass Roots Inc., an ardently pro-dam citizens' group based in Grand Junction, Colorado, demonstrated that just the opposite would in fact be the case. "Far from destroying the scenic and scientific values of this unique area, many of the nation's most respected scientists, artists, sportsmen and travelers feel that Echo Park Dam will actually enhance the Dinosaur Monument area."[22]

There was one final card that the dam's supporters had in hand, one which they never thought they would have to play. Written into the 1938 Presidential Proclamation creating the expanded Dinosaur National Monument was a provision stating that any existing power and reclamation land withdrawals, or reservations, would be unaffected by the proclamation. This provision, in the eyes of the supporters, left the Monument open to development. There were dozens of such withdrawals, dating as far back as 1904.[23] Besides what they considered common sense and the good of the nation, the pro-dam groups had the force of law on their side. The fate of Echo Park seemed to be sealed.

Unfortunately for the plans of the loose coalition of groups supporting the dam, there were others who did not share their positive view. First among these was the National Park Service. To this agency, created about the same time as the original Dinosaur National Monument, their mandate was clear:

The service . . . shall promote and regulate the use of the national parks, [and] monuments . . . by such measures as conform to the fundamental purpose of the said parks . . . which purpose is to conserve the scenery and the natural and historical objects therein and to provide for the enjoyment of the same in such manner and by such means as will leave them unimpaired for the enjoyment of future generations.[24]

This left no room for seven-hundred-foot concrete arch dams in a national monument. The Park Service was under intense pressure from its parent agency, the Department of the Interior, which also included the Bureau of Reclamation, to give the project its blessing. In a report published in 1950, the Park Service made their position quite clear:

The dam would be totally alien to the geology and landscape of the monument. It would be . . . from the viewpoint of monument values, a lamentable intrusion. . . . Particularly deplorable effects of the Echo Park Reservoir would occur in the localities of Pat's Hole and Echo Park. . . .[25]

The National Park Service found a ready ally in their opposition to the dam in the conservation movement. By the end of World War II, this movement was just over half a century old, and for a good part of its history it had been ineffective, wracked by schisms between the conservationist and preservationist factions. These two differing philosophies were embodied in, respectively, Gifford Pinchot, chief forester under Theodore Roosevelt, and John Muir, noted author, naturalist, early advocate of wilderness preservation, and founder of the Sierra Club. The former believed in wise management of the public lands to provide for a continuous supply of water, minerals, and timber—the forerunner of the concept of multiple use—while Muir and his followers believed in the preservation of lands for their aesthetic and spiritual values, a more difficult idea to get across to pragmatic Americans.

The preservationists were stirred by bitter memories of the loss in 1914 of the beautiful Hetch Hetchy Valley in Yosemite National Park to a similar water-storage project for San Francisco. The threat to Dinosaur National Monument and therefore to the entire park system, however, brought the conservation movement together in a united front to defeat the dam. This time, they vowed, the "needs of the people" and even the shibboleth of National Defense be damned. There would not be such an intrusion in a national park again.[26]

As the time for the congressional hearings on the Colorado River Storage Project drew near, battle lines were drawn. Each side called in its expert witnesses, its supporters in Congress and the Cabinet, and for the anti-dam forces, an army of letter writers. The opponents of the dam consisted of a coalition of conservation groups led by David Brower, head of the Sierra Club, and included the Sierra Club, the Wilderness Society, the National Wildlife Federation, the Audubon Society, and the Izaak Walton League. They received unexpected aid from the Lower Basin states, Nevada and California, who felt that all of the water in the Colorado River system had already been allocated by the Colorado River Compact of 1922, and any further storage projects would only take away water they felt was rightfully theirs. An unexpected and surprising ally was Utah's independent governor, J. Bracken Lee. Lee was no environmentalist, but he was an ardent fiscal conservative and was adamantly opposed to any big, expensive government project, no matter what the supposed benefits.[27]

Another member of the anti-dam coalition, and a very important one as it turned out, was the National Geographic Society. *National Geographic* was read and respected by millions of Americans. To show that river running was a pastime that could be enjoyed by anyone, the society and the Sierra Club sponsored river trips down the Green and the Yampa. The resulting articles and photographs graphically demonstrated the beauty of the canyon country and did much to dispel the image of Dinosaur as an inaccessible no-man's land that could only be seen by the daring or foolhardy.

Noted authors such as Wallace Stegner and Bernard DeVoto joined the anti-dam forces, lending their prestige and writing and editing skills to the publications produced by the conservationist coalition. Wildlife experts testified that flooding the canyons would ruin delicate riparian habitats, while archaeologists pointed out that irreplaceable ancient dwellings and artifacts would be lost forever.

All of these were side issues, however. The main thing at stake in the controversy, in the eyes of dam opponents, was the principle of the inviolability of the national parks. They viewed the national parks as preserves, set aside just as they were, in perpetuity for the enjoyment and edification of future generations. It made no difference to them that the 1938 proclamation had specifically set aside the damsites for future reclamation projects. In the opinion of the anti-dam coalition, any plan allowing a dam in Dinosaur National Monument would set a very dangerous precedent, opening the door for development of any sort in any national park. The future and the concept of the national park system was at stake.

Supporters of the project didn't see matters in this light at all. To them, it was purely a western issue, as reclamation and storage projects had always been, and no business of the preservationists from California and the East Coast.[28] They failed to recognize just how deep the feelings of their opponents ran. That failure was to be their first, and ultimately fatal, mistake.

Initially, it seemed that the project would breeze through Congress. Most of the congressional delegations from the western states, virtually every state and local official, as well as high cabinet officials, many federal bureau heads, and the president himself were avid supporters of the plan, including the Echo Park Dam. Business lobbies and citizens' groups lobbied for quick passage of the bill authorizing the construction of the dams. With such support, the pro-dam forces felt, how could they lose?

As the lengthy and often acrimonious hearings dragged on into the 1950s, however, it became apparent to the advocates of the Echo Park Dam that the controversy was eroding support for the entire project. One by one, those who had at first supported the Echo Park unit began to defect. By this time, ardent backers of the embattled dam realized that they were up against a national movement to thwart their plans, and enlisted pro-dam experts, scientists, and authors and organized their own letter-writing campaigns. It was too late. Wherever the supporters of the dam went to seek allies, they found that their opponents had been there before them. Pressure began to mount in Congress to drop the Echo Park Dam from the enabling legislation, and soon the Utah delegation found itself alone in its continued support. Debate grew ever more heated as the pro-dam side found its coalition falling apart; tempers flared and witnesses were sometimes ejected from committee rooms. The flustered chairman of the House Subcommittee on Irrigation and Reclamation declared at one point, "Good taste has no place in these hearings."[29] By this point, supporters of the dam found that their unbending, heated arguments for its construction were in fact having the opposite effect: they alienated and embarrassed those more moderate members of Congress who until then were on their side.

Senate Bill 500, authorizing funding of the Colorado River Storage Project, passed the Senate in April 1955 with the Echo Park Dam authorization intact.[30] Proponents believed that the long fight was over and that victory was at hand. Supporters in the House, however, realized that the bill would never pass that body if the legislation contained authorization for the controversial dam. Opponents of the project saw this as a chance to defeat the entire bill. Congressional observers were treated to the spectacle of both sides suddenly reversing their positions, with its former supporters asking that the Echo Park Dam be dropped from the bill and its opponents calling for its retention.[31] Finally, strategists in the House were able to have the authorization of the Echo Park Dam deferred until a later date so that the vote on the less controversial units of the project could proceed. That done, the bill passed the House by a comfortable margin on 1 March 1956, and was signed as Public Law 485 by President Eisenhower on 11 April, scarcely a month later.

Proponents of the Echo Park Dam, believing congressional promises that the project would still be considered, tried repeatedly throughout the rest of the 1950s and well into the 1960s to have the bill reintroduced. Each time, however, they met with defeat in Congress. It finally became apparent to even the most diehard supporters that the idea of a great dam in Echo Park would never pass.[32] Conservationists, flushed with success, congratulated each other and hailed the defeat of the dam as a great victory for the concept of wilderness and for the national park ideal. Hetch Hetchy had been avenged.

In the cities and small towns of the Intermountain West, however, the defeat left a bitter taste. The supporters of the project, once so confident of success, were shocked and stunned. Many felt betrayed by Congress, especially by those members who had at first pledged to work for authorization of the dam and then had defected when the pressure got too great. Some blamed the National Park Service, the conservationists, and the legislatures of California and Arizona. In this era of McCarthyism and red scares, some felt that the defeat was a Communist plot to weaken national defense.

Part of the blame for the defeat of the project, however, must lie with the supporters of the dam. When opposition to the dam began to grow, they mistakenly believed that it was a manifestation of a jurisdictional dispute between the Park Service and the Bureau of Reclamation. They failed entirely to realize that they were up against a nationwide, grass-roots movement. By the time the supporters realized just what they were facing, it was too late. For some residents of the states, whose dreams of prosperity were shattered by the defeat of the dam, the memory remains an unpleasant one.[33]

Wherever blame or credit may lie, the fact remains that the defeat of the Echo Park Dam was a landmark in the ongoing struggles between conservationists and developers. The forces of the conservation movement were immeasurably strengthened by the victory, emboldened by its success. Many of the lessons learned by both sides were put to use in the conservation battles of the 1960s and 1970s. For the first time, the Iron Triangle of western water interests, the Bureau of Reclamation, and Congress, had seen a proposed water storage project defeated and had been forced to accept a compromise.

For compromise there was. Like most battles over the environment, there were no winners or losers, only bargainers. In order to save Echo Park and, by extension, the national park system, another canyon had to be sacrificed. Nor were Echo Park and Dinosaur National Monument left completely unscarred by the controversy. In the process of raising the public consciousness about the rivers and the park, the Green and the Yampa became household words. Visitation to the hitherto largely unknown region increased dramatically and found the National Park Service unprepared for such an influx. River runners rose from less than one thousand per year before the controversy made the headlines to almost ten thousand by the end of the 1960s.[34] In the first part of the 1970s, faced with mounting accumulations of trash, trampled riverbanks, and overcrowding both on the river and at campsites, the Park Service set a limit on the number of people annually allowed on the river. Numbers of commercial operators who could hold permits or concessions were frozen. Was it worth it, then? Only those who have floated the Green and the Yampa or camped under the cliffs at Echo Park are sure of their answers.

Except for more visitors, the controversy had little actual effect on the canyons of the Green. With congressional authorization and funding, the Bureau of Reclamation wasted no time. In July 1956, the first workmen moved onto the Flaming Gorge damsite, which originally was to have been called Ashley Dam. How did the dam at Flaming Gorge survive the congressional wars that had killed the Echo Park Dam? The upper canyons of the Green were just as beautiful, just as rich in history, but they weren't protected by a national park boundary. Instead of the entire country being affected by the loss of a national monument,

U.S. Bureau of Reclamation surveyor overlooking Flaming Gorge damsite, about 1958.

the only loss in the case of the Flaming Gorge Dam, it seemed, was to a few ranchers, farmers, and sheepmen.

On 15 October 1956, President Eisenhower in the White House set off by remote control the first blasts to begin the excavation of the footings for the dam.[35] The construction contract for the dam and powerhouse was awarded to the Arch Dam Constructors, a consortium of construction companies from the Midwest, in January 1957. On 19 November 1959, the completed diversion tunnel was opened and for the first time in millions of years, the Green was turned out of its ancient channel. On 30 September 1960, the first concrete for the dam was poured, and from then on the rise of the structure was slow but inexorable. By the middle of 1961, almost 100,000 cubic yards of concrete had been poured. By the end of the year, the figure had climbed to almost half a million cubic yards. On 30 October 1962, the diversion tunnel was closed and the waters of the Green began to back up behind the uncompleted dam. One of the first things to be inundated was the treacherous Ashley Falls, which was only about two miles upstream from the damsite. As the waters rose, they covered the Manila-to-Linwood bridge, forcing closure of the highway and construction of a temporary suspension bridge to link the two towns. The last bucket of concrete was poured on 15 November 1962. President Kennedy threw a switch in Salt Lake City to start the first generator, and commercial power generation began on 11 November 1963 at 7 A.M.

Much work remained to be done: clearing the trees and debris from below the high-water mark, completing the two other generators, building roads around the filling reservoir, and constructing a visitors' center at the dam. The dam, however, was complete. Water was rising behind the closed floodgates, power was flowing to distant cities.

In dollars and cents, the dam, power plant, switchyard and "appurtenant structures" had cost $65,297,407.[36] By another method of reckoning, five men had paid for the dam with their lives, three in accidents involving the machinery used in its construction, one in a fall, and one by drowning.[37] The taxpayers had received for their $65 million a thin-arch, concrete dam 502 feet high, 1,285 feet across the top, and 151 feet wide at the base. It contains almost a million cubic yards of concrete, and has three 52,000-horsepower generators that produce 36,000 kilowatts each. The reservoir is ninety-one miles long, backing up almost to the town of Green River, Wyoming and close to 500 feet deep next to the dam. It has a storage capacity of 3,789,000 acre-feet.[38]

There were other costs too. The history beneath the still waters of the reservoir was incalculable and is a permanent loss. While this is an abstract cost, to be sure, it is one that should be considered before undertaking such a project. This buried history is all too often forgotten and passes quickly from the minds of the public and the engineers, living on in only a few fading memories.

The little town of Linwood, now crumbling beneath the reservoir, survives only in photographs, newspaper clippings, and the memories of a few former residents. Built around the turn of the century, Linwood became a trade center for the many cattle and sheep ranches in the Lucerne Valley. A ferry and a narrow bridge crossed the river, and there were a couple of stores and some homes. Among the latter was the cabin built in the 1840s by Uncle Jack Robinson, a mountain man and companion of Jim Bridger. The Linwood school was a unique structure, one that gained the town some measure of momentary fame by being situated exactly on the Utah-Wyoming line. Linwood was not a big town, but it was quiet and picturesque, graced by many tall cotton-woods, from which it got its name. More than that, it was home.

When the reservoir began to fill, Uncle Jack's cabin and the school building were moved to higher ground and saved. The regulations of the Bureau of Reclamation, however, specified that everything not re-moved had to be destroyed and nothing could remain standing below the maximum pool elevation. The cottonwood trees and willows were cut down. The Smith-Larsen Mercantile Store, in business since 1909, was burned. So were the barns, the corrals, the fences, and the remaining homes. Minnie Crouse Rasmussen, daughter of Charlie Crouse of Browns Park fame, refused to let the Bureau of Reclamation crew any-where near her house. Instead, she set it on fire herself, and watched, tears in her eyes, as the flames consumed her home of fifty years.[39]

In place of Linwood, there is the modern town of Dutch John, erected almost overnight by the government in the late 1950s as a home for the thousands of workers who built the dam. Before that, Dutch John Flat was a desolate sagebrush plain inhabited only by coyotes, rabbits, and an occasional vulture. It was named for Dutch John Honse-lena, a hermit and horse trader who lived around the area in the 1860s. At its peak, the new town had a population of about 3,500. Today it houses only about three hundred people, mostly employees of the For-est Service or the Bureau of Reclamation and their families.[40]

Flaming Gorge is one of Utah's most popular vacation spots, sec-ond only to Lake Powell as a center for boating, water skiing, and fish-ing. The largest trout in the state are taken with regularity from its deep green waters. The reservoir and surrounding areas were declared a na-tional recreation area by President Johnson in 1968. At that time, a group of Wyoming businessmen and politicians tried to have it renamed Lake O'Mahoney, after one of the dam's early supporters, Senator Joseph O'Mahoney of Wyoming. Historical usage prevailed, and the present name was made official by proclamation.[41] In an all-too-rare display of intergovernmental cooperation, the National Park Service relinquished control of the national recreation area to the U.S. Forest Service. Since Flaming Gorge N.R.A. is surrounded on all sides by the Ashley Na-tional Forest, the change in administration was logical and has greatly simplified administration.[42]

The cold waters have had a serious effect on the fish that live in the river. The humpback chub and Colorado River squawfish, once so abundant, are gone, replaced by stocked trout in the 1960s.[43] At first, the trout flourished in the clear waters, making the river below the dam a fisherman's paradise. For some reason, in the late 1970s the trout began to die off and those that survived would not reproduce. It was theorized that the discharge from the depths of the reservoir was too cold and insufficient in oxygen for the fish to live. How they had lived during the previous decade was not explained by the theory, but the Bureau of Reclamation, or the Water and Power Resources Board, as it was by then called, decided that the situation was ruining its image with fishermen. In 1979 a small fortune was spent to build shutters on top of the dam that would bring water from the top of the reservoir and mix it with the discharge from the turbines, in the hope of raising the temperature and thereby improving the fish habitat. Whether it works or not has yet to be seen.[44]

The Green has also been drastically affected far downstream. The once-feared rapids of Lodore are now, during low-release periods, little more than rock gardens with the remnants of the river trickling through them. This has had a curious psychological effect on river runners. Lodore has come to be considered nothing more than an easy run, good training for novice boatmen. The Yampa, in turn, was once considered an exciting, but certainly not dangerous run. This situation was changed literally overnight by a flash flood in June 1965 which created Warm Springs Rapid. Warm Springs, described as a Grand Canyon-sized rapid on a medium-sized river, has made the Yampa one of the most demanding runs on the Colorado River system.

As a result of the unusually high run-off and consequently high releases from the dam during the spring of 1983, the Green surprised many river runners. While the Bureau of Reclamation had been releasing as little as 800 cubic feet per second (cfs) from the dam in previous years, during that season they were forced to let out as much as 12,000 cfs. Many unsuspecting rafters flipped their boats or lost them altogether in the re-invigorated rapids. A generation of boatmen who had grown up on the low flows were suddenly made aware of why Lodore had had such a fearsome reputation in the old days. This reprieve for the canyon and the river are no doubt temporary, however; as soon as the water level in the reservoir drops, the river will once again be reduced to a trickle, muttering over the rocks like an old man lost in his memories.

The taming of the river has not been without its positive aspects. For a few small towns and businesses near the reservoir, the dam has proven to be no less than economic salvation. Before the dam, there was only a rough dirt road leading from Vernal over the mountain to Manila, Utah. To facilitate construction, and as part of the deal, the Bureau of Reclamation financed Utah 44, an excellent all-weather road. Manila owes its continued existence to the income derived from the fishermen and boaters who flock to Flaming Gorge Reservoir. The benefits have spilled over into communities as far away as Rock Springs, Wyoming, as well as Vernal, Utah, both of which proclaim themselves the "Gateway to Flaming Gorge."

After the gates of the dam closed in 1963, the regulated flow of the Green meant that the river could be run at virtually any time of year. The hazards of high water during spring run-off and the exposed rocks in the channel during the summer and fall were nearly eliminated, or at least minimized, by the dam. It did not take long for a few adventurous outfitters, some old, some new, to realize this fact and capitalize on it. After so many years of people running the Green for adventure, now more were starting to run the river for the reason that brought General Ashley to it in the first place. There was money to be made.

9

Making a Living

It is a basic fact of American life that whenever enough people start enjoying something, someone else will figure out a way to make a living from it. Even among today's noncommercial river runners, the talk around the campfire almost invariably leads to the questions: Why go back to our dull jobs? Why not do this for a living? This is not so farfetched; virtually every one of the many commercial river outfitters started out running rivers for sport.

It is no longer easy to become a commercial outfitter. In Dinosaur National Monument, which includes Lodore, the Yampa, Whirlpool, and Split Mountain canyons, only thirteen concessionaires, or licensed river guides who hold National Park Service concessions, are allowed to operate; only eleven of these permits are currently in use. In order to take passengers down the river for money, the aspiring outfitter must buy out one of the existing river companies. The companies do not come up for sale often, and they are not cheap. The cost for boats, equipment, the concession, and user-days can run into tens of thousands of dollars. Back in the old days, though, before the Park Service put limits on the number of outfitters, things were different. If a man wanted to become a river outfitter, all he needed was a boat or two and a couple of willing and adventurous passengers.

Naturally enough, the origins of commercial river running are in dispute. Any number of companies claim that they were the first. Outfitters were taking paying customers down the rivers of the northwest as early as the 1920s, but these were hunting and fishing trips—means to an end.[1] About everyone involved in the business today concedes that the first commercial river running as we know it began on the Green, in Flaming Gorge, Red Canyon, Lodore. The pioneer was a local Vernal man named Bus Hatch.

Bus was born in Vernal in 1907 and grew up around the Green River. As a boy, he and his friends would float through the rapids of Split Mountain on "old inner tubes and logs . . . just as kids would." To make extra money for the family, he built a seine and would take fish from the river, haul them to Vernal in gunnysacks, and sell them for chicken feed and fertilizer.

When he got older, Bus became a carpenter. It was only natural that he would eventually apply his skills to making a boat, although by all accounts his first one wasn't much of a success. He built it out of unseasoned lumber and after a few hours in the water, it fell apart and left him swimming. Bus was a fine carpenter, but to produce good boats he needed good advice.[2]

Bus's boyhood friend was Frank Swain.[3] Besides being the undertaker in Vernal, Frank was the deputy sheriff. In 1931 he was sent down to La Sal, Utah, near Moab, to pick up a prisoner for nonsupport of his family and bring him back to the county jail in Vernal. The prisoner was Parley Galloway, son of Nathaniel Galloway. Back in the jail, Parley told Frank and Bus stories of running the river with his father and with Clyde Eddy, a frustrated filmmaker whom Parley had guided through the Grand Canyon in 1927. He told the two friends that Eddy owed him money and if they would get it and bail him out of jail, he would show them how to build a good boat and take them down the Green himself.

Frank and Bus arranged for Parley to be set free on bail, whereupon he promptly disappeared and was not seen in the Uinta Basin again. They didn't need him anyway, they decided; Bus could build the boat and they would go down the river on their own. And down the river they went, Bus and Frank and a couple of friends: no life jackets, no waterproof bags, just their provisions and bedrolls in a gunny sack tied to the side of the boat. Even though they had learned how to make good boats, however, they hadn't learned how to use them. On the first trip,

Bus rowed facing upstream, and one of the boats was capsized and lost in Red Canyon. All their provisions went with it; they were left with an onion and a few potatoes and their rifles. A lucky shot got them some venison, and they finished the trip in good shape. They learned from their mistakes, however, and within the next couple of years, they were taking boats all the way down the Green, through the Grand Canyon, and even down the Salmon River in Idaho.

In one respect, Bus Hatch was no different from all the later commercial outfitters: his business started out as a cost-sharing venture. He wanted to get on the river, and the more people he could interest in going, the more trips he could take. Money was hard to come by in those Depression years, and if there was a little cash left over at the end of the trip, so much the better. But if they had a flat tire on the way to the launch, or lost an oar on the river, he would lose money. Clearly things needed to be on a sound financial basis.

One regular passenger on Bus's prewar trips was Dr. Russell Frazier of Bingham, Utah. Frank Swain had met the doctor previously, and Frazier had gotten him a job at the copper mine near Bingham, Utah. The doctor had been interested in river running, but didn't know much about boats and rivers. He did have one thing that Bus didn't, however: cash. Frazier went on a number of trips with Bus and Frank in the 1930s, including the Grand Canyon in 1934 and the Middle Fork of the Salmon in 1936.[4]

In those days it was hard to make a living running a river company for a number of reasons. People didn't have money to spend on such frivolities, and not that many people outside of eastern Utah had ever heard of the Green River. The river itself still had the reputation of being a place where a person was lucky to get out alive. The simplest reason, however, had to do with the Galloway boat. It was a fine craft for navigating fast water, but it would not hold enough passengers to make it pay. There was room for the oarsman and one, or at the most two, passengers sitting on the front and rear decks. When they came to rapids, the passengers were just about forced to walk around, or if they wanted to stay in the boat, to cling desperately to the deck. It wasn't until the advent of inflatable rubber boats that running rivers on a commercial scale became feasible.

No matter the difficulties, by 1936 Bus and Frank were "piloting dudes" on ten-day commercial trips from Green River to Jensen.[5] The charge for one of these trips was about $65, or $6.50 per day. By this

time Bus's two sons, Don and Ted, were old enough to go along on
some of the trips. Don, born in 1928, recalls that as a youngster he
didn't see much of the river:

> I don't remember when I wasn't running trips. . . . My earliest recollec-
> tion was when I was too little to sit right in the boat . . . I'd lay in the
> bottom of the boat and hang on—right flat in the bottom so I wouldn't
> get thrown out. . . . I didn't see the canyon until I grew up a little bit
> bigger. I was always laying in the bottom holding on to something.[6]

The business became even more of a family affair in 1939, when
Bus took his wife, Eva, and his friends Wes Eddington and Roy DeSpain
and their wives down the Yampa in three boats.

Down to the south, on the San Juan River, Norman Nevills of Mexican Hat, Utah, was beginning to give Bus some competition. Legend
has it that he built his first boat out of the boards from an old outhouse.
By 1938 he had developed his own style of boat, which he called a cataract boat and others called a sadiron skiff. It was similar in design
to the Galloway boats except that the bow as well as the stern was squared
off and it was somewhat wider.[7] Depending on who you talked to, it
worked just about as well, although Don Hatch says that Nevills's boats
tended to capsize more easily in a big hole.

Nevills's first commercial trip was in 1938, when he took two
University of Michigan botanists, Dr. Elzada Clover and Lois Jotter,
from Green River, Utah, to Lee's Ferry. The two women were the first
commercial passengers to ever float the Green. Aside from capsizing
a boat in Cataract Canyon, the trip was a success. Two years later, in
1940, he was ready to try the upper canyons. Before starting down the
river, however, he stopped for advice and directions from the man who
was by now known as the one to ask about running the Green: Bus Hatch.

Nevills started on 20 June 1940, from Green River, Wyoming, on
a "well-publicized commercial trip";[8] paying passengers included Senator Barry Goldwater, who joined the party at Green River, Utah. At
Echo Park, the Nevills group ran into two men who had started down
the canyons a few days before them. They were old river-rat Bert Loper
and a newcomer, Don Harris. In a wooden boat of Loper's manufac-
ture, they had run all the way from Green River Lakes in the Wind
River Mountains of Wyoming.[9]

Both parties stopped at Vernal for a Fourth of July celebration. Nevills and his passengers went on down the river, all the way through the Grand Canyon to Lake Mead. Loper and Harris, who was soon to start his own river company specializing in up-river jetboat trips, went only as far as Jensen. They were back the next July for a trip down the Yampa. Loper and Harris planned other trips, too, but before the canyons saw another spring rise, the country had been plunged into World War II.

There was not much in the way of river running during the war. Everyone was either in the armed forces or too busy working in defense plants to take the time. In 1942, however, around the end of May, Bus Hatch led a party that consisted of David Lanfield, superintendent of Rocky Mountain National Park, plus scientists and biologists from the National Park Service, the University of Colorado, and the Smithsonian Institution. This distinguished crew, a far cry from the usual slightly disreputable river runners, was conducting a survey of the resources of Dinosaur National Monument. They started from Sunbeam, Colorado, floating down the Yampa to its confluence with the Green, and on down to Jensen. They inspected the Indian ruins and petroglyphs along the Yampa, possible damsites on the Green, and the dinosaur bone quarry near Jensen.[10]

A story told around Vernal has it that Bus and a brother, C. L., or Tom, as he was known, took some time off from their jobs in a defense plant for some river running. Looking for a place that was nearby but that they hadn't tried before, they decided on Cross Mountain Gorge, on the Yampa above Lily Park. The Park Service party had hauled their boats around this short, but steep and rugged gorge, and Bus wanted to see what it was like. They stopped to ask a rancher for directions to the head of the canyon, but he told them instead that they were crazy to try it—they would never get out of the canyon alive. Bus had run the Green, the Colorado, and the Salmon, though, and felt pretty sure of his skills as a boatman. They ignored the old stockman's warnings and headed for the top of the canyon.

A few days later, a couple of half-naked, battered, bruised and humbled boatmen came stumbling back into the little town of Cross Mountain, Colorado. The two brothers had lost their boats in the first waterfall, and had been forced to climb out of the canyon and hike across

Early Hatch River Expeditions pontoon rig in Triplet Falls.

the sagebrush to the highway. As good as they were, this time the Hatches had met their match.[11]

World War II was fought in deserts and mountains, rural country-side and steaming jungles, city streets and isolated islands. The many environments the war was waged in required the development of new kinds of equipment. One specialized item was the inflatable bridge pontoon. Pontoon bridges had been used by armies since the time of Xerxes, but the difference was that this particular type could be rolled up and transported to where it was needed, and then simply inflated. A string of these pontoons would be lashed together side by side and a temporary bridge built over them. They were made out of rubberized canvas, tough and heavy, and came in various sizes.

Another piece of equipment developed for the military during the war was the assault raft. This inflatable craft was also made of rubber-ized canvas, and was about fourteen feet long by six feet wide, although they were not all the same size. The standard raft could carry ten fully equipped soldiers, or about two thousand pounds. They were used for river crossings, beach assaults, or landing infiltration teams on hostile shores, and were also very tough and very heavy.

When the war ended, production of war material was at its peak. The armed forces were left with huge stocks of everything: four-engined bombers, pistols, tanks, bridge pontoons, and assault rafts. The surplus was shipped to property distribution centers around the country and sold below cost. The pontoons and rafts, for example, sold for as little as twenty-five dollars each. There was one such depot in Salt Lake City.

It's hard to say just who was the first to come up with the idea of using surplus rafts and pontoons for running rivers. Like so many good ideas, it seems that a number of people came up with it at the same time. John Cross, who at the end of the war was working for the Boy Scouts of America, was one to see the possibilities for scouting.[12] He thought a river adventure would be just the thing for the scouts, and in seeking some suitable craft, heard about the surplus sales. At first, the scout leaders considered buying about a hundred navy one-man life rafts that came fully equipped with flares, sail, distillation kit, and emergency food, for one dollar each. The thought of hundreds of scouts strung up and down the river, however, caused them to reconsider. Instead, they settled on ten brand new navy ten-man life rafts, similar to the army's assault rafts but also provided with emergency equipment. These cost the Boy Scout Council $250. They were quickly put to use on trips down Glen Canyon, and some of them stayed in service for years.

Bus Hatch was another to quickly recognize the possibilities of inflatable craft for the outfitter. He picked up a number of thirty-three-foot bridge pontoons for twenty-five dollars each, built a wooden frame, added two sets of oars, and he was in business. Here at last was a way to make a living running rivers. The modified bridge pontoons could carry a large load of passengers and do it in relative safety. All he needed now were customers.

They came soon enough, and from an unlikely source. As the controversy over the Echo Park Dam heated up after the war, places like Echo Park, the Yampa, and Lodore, suddenly were splashed across the pages of national magazines. Both sides of the issue sponsored river trips. The anti-dam side wanted to increase public awareness of the beauties found along the rivers and to demonstrate that the canyons were not just for the adventurous, but for everyone. The pro-dam people wanted to show that only daredevils and the foolhardy would venture

down the treacherous Green River. Groups that supported the dam found
in some cases that their pamphlets describing the Green as the "most
dangerous river in the world" had the opposite effect. Many were
intrigued and sensed that here was something lacking in post-war, subur-
banized America: adventure. The result was a greater awareness of the
Green and the Yampa than ever before. Bus Hatch suddenly had more
business than he could handle.[13]

Others were not slow to move in. Norm Nevills, for example, continued to run an occasional trip on the Green, although his usual haunts
were the San Juan River, Glen Canyon, and the Grand Canyon. Nevills
kept his wooden boats, too, after most other companies had gone to
inflatable rafts. Nevills's last trip on the Green, and indeed one of his
last river trips, was from Green River to Jensen in June 1949.[14] The
passengers, including five women, rode in four cataract boats. This con-
stituted the largest number of women who had ever been down the river
at one time. The trip started from Green River on 20 June 1949 after
a ceremony dedicating the Powell Monument at Expedition Island, where
Norm Nevills was presented with special license plates for his boats
by the highway departments of Utah and Wyoming. Nevills didn't make
any more runs down the Green. He and his wife were killed later that
same year when their light plane crashed near Mexican Hat, Utah.

Another outfitter who started his business right after the war was
the eccentric Harry Aleson. Aleson was already well known among river
runners for twice swimming the lower Grand Canyon with Georgie
White. He had started in the river business during the war in a short-
lived partnership with Norm Nevills. Norm could be hard to get along
with, however, and it wasn't until Aleson started a partnership with
his friend and financial backer Charles Larabee that he was able to make
a living running rivers. Larabee was able to buy a number of surplus
assault rafts, and with Aleson's enthusiasm and his partner's business
sense, Larabee and Aleson Western River Tours was on the water.[15]
Aleson usually ran the Colorado through Glen Canyon. He had been
an aviator in World War I and had been shot down and gassed. As a
consequence, he suffered from a ruined stomach for the rest of his life.
He could eat only bland foods, and the adrenalin and jittery nerves caused
by running rapids like those on the upper Green and in the Grand Canyon, for instance, caused him agony. He did run quite a few trips on
the Green, usually for pleasure. A typical example is one that he made
with his friend Pete Sparkes in August of 1951.

Norm Nevills and Joe Desloge in Ashley Falls 24 June 1949.

They started on 9 August from Green River, and stopped just below the town to visit with Eva Holmes, who had lived at her ranch by the river since 1910. "Here is a grand character," Aleson wrote. "She has seen all the river parties to come this way . . . the Kolb brothers in 1911; the U.S.G.S. Survey of 1916, the French kayak party (deColmont) . . . Buzz Holmstrom, 1937, and in 1938, Holmstrom and Amos Burg; in 1940 Nevills exp."

Aleson was insatiably curious, stopping at every mark on the wall of the canyon and every pile of rocks. At Ashley Falls, his curiosity paid off. "We look over all likely boulders, low and high," for the inscription left by the fur trader a century and a quarter before. After finding inscriptions left by many other river parties, his persistence was rewarded:

> On the face of a [boulder] . . . facing toward the river . . . is a lichen-splashed area with portions of a perfect and plain A. Black lichen in the grooves. Light-colored rock stands sharply out to form the small triangle in top of the A. A shallow groove can be followed by finger tips. The[re] is proper space to hold the other 4 letters. Below, indistinct markings could have been the date.[16]

This was a find of major historical importance, and it is fortunate that Aleson was able to record it on film before the site was covered by Flaming Gorge Reservoir less than ten years later.

Aleson's commercial trips were first class and known for fine food. This was probably a consequence of his bad stomach. His stomach pains did not stop him from enjoying the finer things of life, however: "Aug. 16 . . . from 5:30 on, this old river boatman enjoyed the cocktail hour. How? A cup of cool Green River water, diluted with a generous jigger of 151 proof Hudson Bay rum."[17]

Aleson's run of Lodore, Whirlpool Canyon, and Split Mountain was routine; the rapids that had so terrified earlier travelers he described merely as "sporting." When he got to Vernal, he visited the local cemetery to find the graves of Nathaniel Galloway and his wife. When he saw the dilapidated condition of their grave markers, he made new ones of wood and later paid for marble stones for both of them. Aleson himself did not last too much longer; when Glen Canyon Dam was built and flooded his beloved canyon, it took the heart out of him. The canyon's death preceded his own by only a few years.

All of this activity on the river did not go unnoticed, either by the paying passengers—virtually all of the business of commercial outfitters until relatively recently came to them by word of mouth—or by the government. The Park Service, the state of Utah, even the Coast Guard took notice of what was happening on the Green, and much to the disgust of the outfitters, decided that the free and easy days on the river were over.

The first bureaucracy to step in was the state of Utah. The Public Service Commission took alarm at all this unregulated traffic—John Cross reported he "had as many as 350 students out on two or three rivers at one time, on the same day. We had trucks and equipment going in all directions."[18] In 1959 the Utah legislature passed the State Boating Act,[19] which among other things, was the first official notice that river running was becoming a business and needed to be regulated, at least in the eyes of the state authorities. Less that ten years later, the state decided to require all commercial boatmen to obtain a license from the State Parks and Recreation Commission. Next into the act was the Public Service Commission. Since it regulated all other forms of traffic, such as trains, busses, and airlines, regulating commercial boat traffic was logical. Besides the boating permit, the commission now required tour operators to have a bus permit to move their passengers to and from the river. In order to get the necessary permits, the outfitters were now required to have insurance.[20]

The federal government was not far behind. Here was a potential tangle of regulations, because rivers cross so many regulatory boundaries in their courses. On the Green River, the National Park Service, the Bureau of Reclamation, the Bureau of Land Management, the Forest Service, and the Fish and Wildlife Service all claimed jurisdiction. To deal with all of these agencies was impossible and would have soon meant the end of commercial river running. Fortunately, a way through this bureaucratic jungle was found. Since the Green had been declared a navigable river during a court case between the United States and the state of Utah, it was decided that the U.S. Coast Guard had the final say on who regulated whom.[21] This cut across all the other regulatory lines and simplified matters greatly. The Coast Guard required all boatmen to pass a test and obtain a license, which probably did not hurt the safety record of the companies and made a good selling point.

Meanwhile, the number of commercial outfitters continued to grow. Besides Hatch and Harry Aleson, there was Jack Curry, who started

Western River Expeditions around the time that the Echo Park Dam controversy was dying down.[22] He took advantage of the awakened interest in river running and started trips down Lodore in 1961. The prices charged for river tours were slowly going up. Curry charged sixty-five dollars, the same as Bus Hatch and Frank Swain almost thirty years before, but for only four days on the river. At the same time, Hatch River Expeditions, run by Bus and his sons, Don and Ted, held the only concession granted by the Park Service to guide trips through Dinosaur. Curry went to court, claiming that the Hatches had an unfair monopoly, and won the right to also hold a concession.[23] He stayed in the business until 1973, when he sold out to a former partner.

There were others as well, some running what were probably semi-legal, cost-sharing trips, others who just ignored the Park Service and kept on floating the river. Georgie White, who confined most of her river running to the Grand Canyon, ran at least one trip on the upper Green in 1960. About 1950, A. K. Reynolds and Mike Hallacy of Green River, Wyoming, started running commercial tours from Green River to the upper end of Browns Park. Adrian Reynolds, local politician and publisher of the *Green River Star*, had become acquainted with Norm Nevills when Nevills ran the Green in 1947. Adrian's son, A. K., "got the bug" from that acquaintance and asked Norm for the plans to his cataract boats. Nevills complied and Reynolds, his friend Mike Hallacy, and G. G. "Lug" Larson each built one boat. According to one story, Reynolds quit the business when inflatable rafts started becoming popular, claiming that he didn't want to be on the same river with a "baloney boat." His trips were usually for photographers, fishermen, or hunters. Reynolds continued running trips in wooden boats well into the 1960s, when the Green was flooded by Flaming Gorge.[24]

Despite the loss of the upper canyons, commercial river running boomed in the 1960s. In the Grand Canyon, for instance, the number of people running the Colorado jumped from five in 1950 to more than two thousand in 1967.[25] The Green was no different; if anything, there were more people going down the Green than any other western river. Hatch River Expeditions was in the forefront. Besides holding one of the only official concessions, they had built a reputation based on being the pioneer river company and on good service. That reputation still stands, and boatmen who got their start running rivers with Hatch have since branched out into rivers all over the world.

Not everyone who went down the Green in the 1950s was a paying passenger, however. There were still some people who wanted to go on their own, without benefit of a guide. One of these individuals was Les Jones of Heber, Utah. Jones was an adventurous sort, and in September of 1957, he and a friend planned a trip down Lodore in canoes.[26] These were not ordinary canoes, however. They were decked-over aluminum craft, equipped with oars and three watertight compartments. Jones had already been down Lodore a couple of years earlier on a movie-making expedition with a filmmaker named Charles Eggert, and with Don Hatch, Al Galloway, and others.[27] He knew the dangers they would face, but wasn't deterred.

There seemed to be a problem, however. His partner got lost in the maze of obscure dirt roads around the east end of Browns Park before he even got to the river. Jones waited for two days, but his partner never showed up, so he decided to go by himself. Once the decision was made, Jones wasted no time. On Sunday 2 September, he left the Gates of Lodore, ran all of the rapids in Lodore Canyon, stopped to chat with the ranger in Echo Park, and reached Jensen at ten o'clock that same night. This has to be the fastest recorded time anyone has ever navigated the sixty-five miles of canyons and rapids.

The Sierra Club was instrumental in the defeat of the Echo Park Dam, but the end of the threat to Echo Park did not mean the end of the club's interest in the rivers in the area. For many years, the Sierra Club has sponsored trips down the Yampa and the Green. In the early days, before members acquired their own equipment and expertise, the outfitter was usually Bus Hatch. He would take groups of sixty or seventy on week-long trips down Lodore in his dependable pontoon boats. There were almost always a few hardy souls who would accompany the rafts in foldboats, and it would seem that on every trip at least one of the foldboats would end up wrapped around a rock[28] in Disaster Falls or Triplet or S.O.B.[29] Even from its saviors, the river would exact a price.

Another outdoor club that started running trips about the same time was the Wasatch Mountain Club. This organization began in Salt Lake City in 1920, and for the first three decades of its existence, its members were mainly concerned with hiking, mountaineering, and skiing. The club took no official stand on Echo Park Dam, but some of the individual members were active in the defeat of the dam and that must have awakened an interest in the canyons and rivers. In 1957 the club borrowed a couple of pontoon rafts and set off to try running rivers.

One of their first trips, down the Yampa in May 1957, has become something of a legend among club members.[29] A trip down the Yampa in May means gambling with the unpredictable western Colorado weather, and in this case, the club members lost. It rained, turning the clay roads into quagmires. The old bus the club used for trips got stuck several times and the passengers were forced to push it out. The rain turned to hail once they were on the river, and things went from bad to worse. Three people were thrown overboard in Tepee Rapid, the first of any consequence on the Yampa. One of the three, tangled in his poncho, spent a dangerously long time in the cold water and was in pretty bad shape when finally pulled aboard.[30]

This incident, and the continued rain, was enough for eight of the passengers. At the Mantle Ranch, eleven miles above Echo Park, they abandoned the trip and decided instead to make a sixty-mile ride stuffed into the back of Tim Mantle's pickup truck over atrocious roads. The rest of the group, encouraged by improving weather, finished the trip in good shape. The club was not deterred by this inauspicious start and went on to make the Yampa trip an annual event for many years. They also branched out to other rivers, including the Snake, the Salmon, and even the Colorado through Grand Canyon.

Private recreational river running has never been as popular as going with an established company. One of the legacies of the Echo Park Dam controversy was the belief, fostered by the supporters of the dam, and certainly not disputed by the outfitters, that the rivers were too dangerous to float without a guide. During the do-it-yourself era of the 1960s, however, that belief began to change as more and more people bought their own equipment and tried the river themselves. This triggered the formation of a host of new companies manufacturing boats, frames, and safety equipment to meet increasing demand. Today private river runners make up a growing percentage of people on the river.

The number of people going down the river did not escape the watchful eye of the National Park Service, the legal guardians of the Green and the Yampa through Dinosaur National Monument. Popular campgrounds were being trampled, piles of trash accumulated, and the rivers themselves became crowded to the point that there were boat-jams at certain times. The ephemeral quality of a wilderness experience was fading and Park Service planners saw that unless a definite management plan was formulated and acted on, the river was in danger of being loved to death.

After conducting studies in the late 1960s and the early 1970s, the Park Service implemented its Interim River Management Plan in 1972.[31] Under the new guidelines, there would be a limit on the number of people who could go down the river per year, either as passengers or on their own. The requirements for obtaining a commercial concession were tightened, and the number frozen at thirteen. For private river runners, it would now be necessary to obtain a permit by means of an annual lottery. No one really liked the new rules, the commercial outfitters especially, but as the Park Service saw it there was simply no choice.

River running has increased dramatically in popularity over the past decade. In 1973, the year after the river management plan was implemented, Dinosaur reached a high point when over seventeen thousand people floated the rivers—more than ran the Colorado through the Grand Canyon. Two-thirds of them were on commercial trips. In the next ten years, as the regulations were tightened and the nation faced oil embargoes, recessions, and unemployment, the numbers continued to decline. The figure for 1983 was just under ten thousand, which was about evenly split between the outfitters and private river runners. Dinosaur has not really had the tensions between the two groups that have plagued other federally administered rivers, with one group claiming that the rules favor the other. Now, though the numbers of people have declined, there is a solid core of enthusiasts who come back year after year. Permits are increasingly difficult to obtain, indicating that more and more people are applying. There is every indication that the figure will go back up in the future.

Commercial outfitters are optimistic and confident of their future. Many of them are now in the third generation of a family business. They are no longer relying on word of mouth for new business. Outfitters now attend travel shows, apply aggressive marketing techniques, and advertise to recruit new customers. Business is not so bad, either—in Utah alone, the relatively small number of outfitters made over four million dollars in 1982. The figure for the rest of the West was over eight million dollars.[32] New books and articles about river running seem

to appear almost daily, and as more and more people become aware
of the many attractions river running vacations offer besides relatively
low cost—solitude, adventure, challenge, closeness to nature, beauty—it
is likely that the demand will once again begin to increase. As long
as there is a wild river to float, and people to try it, river running as
a business and a sport will be around.

The Green was high that day, swollen by recent floods. The blood-
red canyon walls of Lodore cast a gloomy shadow over the raging maelstrom of waves and spray at their feet. The boatmen were grim as they
faced Hell's Half Mile—they had already lost one boat and almost lost
some of the crew in a wreck at Disaster Falls. This was even worse.
They finally decided it was unrunnable—they would have to make a
portage. First the remaining boats were unloaded, then the supplies and
gear carried around the slippery boulders along the riverside. Next the
heavy boats were carried around the rapid, and all hands breathed a
sigh of relief to see them floating in the calmer waters below. Now
they could move on.

Powell and his crew? Stone, or Galloway, or Todd and Page? No,
this scene did not take place in 1869, or 1909, or 1926. The date was
May 1984, the boaters a group of Boy Scouts on a commercial rafting
trip.[33] The dark and gloomy depths of Lodore had once again proved
to be as much of an obstacle as the rapids themselves. The ghosts of
Ashley, Manly, Bradley, Steward, Bert Loper, and all the others might
have smiled at the sight. Just as the river enters the sea only to return
as rain and snow, so the story of man's use of the Green River had
come full circle. Perhaps things have not changed so much after all.

Tailwaves

The Other "Place No One Knew"

Much has been made among environmentalists of the loss of Glen Canyon to a Bureau of Reclamation project in the early 1960s. Volume after volume has been written about its lost wonders, poems penned, songs composed about the beauties of the canyon forever drowned by the waters of Lake Powell. Radicals agitate for its destruction and even, in fiction at least, hatch plots to accomplish that end. Environmentalists bemoan its fate as their greatest defeat, even though they actually had more than a little to do with that fate.

Glen Canyon was not the only one to be affected by the Colorado River Storage Project, however. At the same time, a sister to Glen Canyon Dam was being built on the Green River, about midway between the town of Green River, Wyoming, and the Uinta Basin. And even though the canyons and river to be inundated were of rare beauty and filled with a rich historical heritage, not a word was said when the gates of Flaming Gorge Dam were closed and the Green began to back up. The salvage survey conducted for Glen Canyon produced shelves of documents, thousands of photographs and hundreds of feet of movie film; Flaming Gorge, Horseshoe, Kingfisher, and Red Canyons rated one fifty-page document. No songs, no films, no poems, no radicals plotting its destruction.

What follows, then, are some descriptions of this stretch of the Green
River as it was in the days before the Green was known as a trout fish-
ery and Flaming Gorge a playground for motorboats. This is not to moan
or complain or bewail the fate of the Green, for the dam is a fact and
given the state of the world will probably be holding back the Green
long after man has reduced himself to ashes. This is simply a reminder
that there was once a river below those cold, green waters; that Glen
Canyon was not the only "place no one knew."

Just below this fork (Henry's Fork) we entered the mouth of the first canyon and encamped amid the cottonwood trees surrounded by bluffs 1200
ft. high and on one side nearly perpendicular. It is the grandest scenery
I have found in the mountains and I am delighted with it. I went out to
see the country this morning and found it grand beyond conception. The
river winds like a serpent through between nearly perpendicular cliffs 1200
ft. high but instead of rapids it is deep and calm as a lake. It is the most
safe of any part we have yet seen for navigation.
                                              —George Y. Bradley, 1869

On the night of the 30th we camped at a bend of the river, which we called
"Beehive Point," for the appearance of the cliff, on the left side of the
river, rounded to the shape of a dome at the top, and covered with cells
carved by the action of the water during some past age, in which hundreds
of swallows had built their nests of clay. As the swallows flit about the
cliff they look like swarms of bees. . . . Opposite this cliff . . . is a vast
amphitheatre, composed of a succession of terraces . . . each platform
or terrace is built of red sandstone, and the space between them is a gentle
slope clothed in green verdure, and on which a row of pine trees grow
in the arc of a circle and the amphitheatre is painted with alternate bands
of green and red.
                                              —Walter Henry Powell, 1869

From this point (the west cliff of Kingfisher Canyon) had a fine view of
the Green winding around at the base of bright red cliffs to the northwest
with the wooded valley of the Kingfisher Creek [Sheep Creek] and the
crystal stream winding in the midst. . . . Bold rocks of grey sandstone
tower on the right; on the left, crags and rocky slopes with scattered ce-
dars, pinons, and firs. . . . The Kingfisher comes in on the right through
a narrow canyon valley with steep walls, the valley itself filled with alders
and willows completely hiding the creek. Then the creek emerging from
its own canyon meanders across the little park, its banks fringed with willows. The river flows at the foot of the cliff on the left and is hedged

by a border of willows from the meadow on the right. Looking down the river the walls seem almost to close where the river turns to the left around Beehive point.

—John Wesley Powell, 1871

Flaming Gorge hard into view, the right side a dark red flame below in the morning sun with a grey cap of sandstone overtopped with brown, the whole cliff rising to 1000 feet. While on the left the quiet green of a lovely grove of cottonwoods heightened by its contrast the beauty and grandeur of the scene. . . . Kingfisher is a beautiful clear stream that ought to contain trout. When we came to the cliff and looked down its valley I thought it as lovely as we ever saw. . . . The valley is thick with cottonwoods, willows, alders, and box elders. The water is clear of a slight reddish tinge, cold, and where it empties into the Green the color of the two streams is brought into vivid contrast.

—Almon Harris Thompson, 1871

Just below the mouth of Henry's Fork [the river] doubled to the left and we found ourselves between two low cliffs, then in a moment we dashed to the right into the beautiful canyon, with the cliffs whose summit we had seen, rising about 1300 feet on the right, and a steep slope on the left at the base of which was a small bottom covered with all cottonwood trees, whose green shone resplendent against the red rocks. . . . The canyon was surprisingly beautiful and romantic. The river seemed to flow with an impetus it had exhibited nowhere above. . . . At the foot of the right hand wall . . . we beheld our first real rapid, gleaming like a jewel from its setting in the sunlight which fell into the gorge, and it had as majestic a setting as could be desired. For myself I can say that the place appeared the acme of the romantic and picturesque. . . . Flaming Gorge is the gateway, Horseshoe the vestibule, and Kingfisher the ante-chamber to the whole grand series.

—Frederick S. Dellenbaugh, 1871

Passing through Horseshoe . . . we found deep, placid pools, and sheer, light red walls rising about four hundred feet on either side, then sloping back steeply to the tree-covered mountains. . . . [I]n Kingfisher Canyon were a few of the fish-catching birds from which the canyon took its name. There were many of the tireless cliff-swallows scattered all through these canyons, wheeling and darting, ever on the wing. . . . It is a picture to tempt an artist. . . . [L]ittle openings, or parks with no trees, are tinted with a beautiful soft gray; "brownstone fronts" are found in the canyon walls; and a very light green in the willow-leafed cottonwoods at the river's edge. . . . The river glistens in the sunlight, as it winds around the base of the wall on which we stand. . . .

We remained until noon of the following day at Ashley Falls, exploring, repairing, and photographing this picturesque spot. The canyon

walls here dropped down to beautiful, rolling foot-hills eight or nine hundred feet high, tree-covered as before but more open. The diversity of
rocks and hills was alluring.

—Ellsworth L. Kolb, 1911

. . . [T]he north wall of Flaming Gorge, with its vivid hues of red, brown,
and ocher, rises like a huge flame of fire ahead. The gorge . . . forms
a very impressive entrance to the series of canyons below. . . . Through
the Flaming Gorge and Horseshoe Canyon box elder trees are scattered
along each bank where the walls offer any footing and pine trees dot the
slopes, extending down to the water's edge. In places the solid rock walls
are almost vertical and rise several hundred feet above the river. The gray
shades of the rock with the generous sprinkling of pines and the river winding its way between the walls form a constantly changing panorama. . . .
[Kingfisher Canyon] is wonderfully beautiful. The river is like a placid
lake, and the beautifully colored canyon walls with their green trees cling-
ing to the slopes are perfectly reflected in the river as in a huge mirror.

—Ralf R. Woolley, 1922

Flaming Gorge, Horseshoe and Kingfisher canyons were short and rapid-
free, filled with sunshine and songs of countless birds, and with the call
of geese and ducks high overhead. Many deer and beaver could be seen
along the tree-lined shores.

—Buzz Holmstrom, 1938

Below here Red Canyon begins, crags and narrowing rock walls present-
ing a dramatic view synchronized to roaring cataracts. Along the narrow
bottoms are tall western yellow pines. . . .

—Amos Burg, 1938

The countryside continues to be sumptuous. Above all, there was the ar-
rival in front of a pink mountain where debris was strewn with little bushes,
lavender in color and with a trifling of yellow due to the flowers. Then,
all of a sudden, an imposing, mysterious overwhelming wall bright red
and dark, at the same time, without vegetation, none—a face completely
stripped, closed, proud and high, rich in its only substance and which gave
the impression of silent majesty.

A little later, the valley opens up. The view reaches up to a background of wooded mountains. The leaves are already yellow there and
there are spots of bright gold in the middle of a covering alternating from
light to dark green.

—Antoine DeSeyne, 1938

We are all terribly impressed by the unusual beauty of this, Horseshoe
Canyon. Not alone is the change so great from the barren canyons above
here, but this canyon is outstanding.

—Norm Nevills, 1947

Flaming Gorge is very beautiful. It is colored red and yellow with a green-ish tinge. Below Flaming Gorge we encounter a small ripple. Next is Horseshoe Canyon with many pines and rocks looking like they do at the Natural Bridges National Monument. . . . Very brilliant walls between Horseshoe and Kingfisher Canyons. . . . Red Canyon is dark red, stud-ded abundantly with yellow pine trees. . . . The scenery is very spectacular and the rapids, although rocky, do not have any big waves at this stage of water.

—Harry P. Sparkes, 1951

. . . [C]amp was set up in Carter's Canyon [Carter Creek] that afternoon. It was a lovely camp setting with rushing streams of cold water on two sides emptying into the Green. . . . [T]he scenery was picturesque. . . . The weather was ideal, and the waters quite exciting with a variety of rapids and spots of quiet.

—Conee Clemens, 1962

I remember Carter Creek as being a beautiful place where a stream came in there. . . . But the living space was the bottom of the canyon . . . where all the deer were—the animals, the geese and all of these; the wildlife was along the bottom. So when you put the dam there and flooded it, it essentially killed all the living space for animals. There were a lot of animals there. . . . The beauty of the canyons seemed to be the bottom-lands of the river—the immediate bottomlands . . . you take a picture of the canyon the way it was and then—and it's a beautiful picture—and then if you take the scissors and cut off the bottom third, that's what it looks like now.

—Don Hatch, 1984

One characteristic of those canyons—those are probably the most ideal places for beginning river runners to get going. They were fairly big waves [but] easy and straightforward. It was very beautiful. . . . We worried a lot about Ashley Falls but it was pretty simple. . . . A good part of that area was forested. . . . I remember one morning having mist hanging over the canyon, hanging over the forested walls; it was . . . one of the love-lier sights I've seen on the river.

—Cal Giddings, 1984

Notes

CHAPTER ONE

1. Ann Zwinger, *Run, River, Run*, 4.

2. U.S. Department of the Interior, Geological Survey, *The Green River and Its Utilization*, xi. An acre-foot is the standard measure of water storage. It equals the amount of water needed to cover one level acre to a depth of one foot.

3. David Lavender, *Colorado River Country*, 184.

4. Ibid., 183–84.

5. Bernard DeVoto, *Across the Wide Missouri*, 54.

6. Frederick S. Dellenbaugh, *The Romance of the Colorado River*, 67.

7. Ted J. Warner, ed., *The Dominguez–Escalante Journal*, 43.

8. Dale L. Morgan, *Jedediah Smith and the Opening of the West*, 169.

9. Ibid.

10. Laura Evans and Buzz Belknap, *Dinosaur River Guide*, 5. For the most part, the descriptions of the canyons, rapids, and other features are based on the authors' experience. For those sections now submerged by Flaming Gorge Reservoir, oral interviews with persons familiar with the river before the dam were relied on. The Belknap guide was used mainly for mileages.

11. J. W. Powell, *The Exploration of the Colorado River and Its Canyons*, 173.

12. One boatman's legend about Whirlpool Canyon concerns two veteran river guides who were taking a boatload of dudes on their first trip through the canyons. The boatmen had primed their passengers for days, muttering and shaking their heads about the dangers of Greasey Pliers Rapid. (The name commemorates the time another boatman lost that essential tool over the side.) As they approached the rapid, which though easy to run is impressive due to the size of its regular waves, both boatmen, by prearranged signal, screamed "We're not going to make it!" and dove over the side of the boat. In the quiet water below, after the boatmen had ridden through it in their life jackets, they climbed back aboard and the journey was resumed. When the passengers realized that they had been had, some of them were not amused. Neither was the outfitter, who fired both boatmen as soon as he heard what had happened.

13. U.S. Department of the Interior, Geological Survey, *The Green River*, 50.

CHAPTER TWO

1. C. Gregory Crampton, "Humboldt's Utah, 1811," *Utah Historical Quarterly* 26 (July 1958):271.

2. Dale L. Morgan, *The Great Salt Lake*, 116–17.

3. Dale L. Morgan, *Jedediah Smith and the Opening of the West*, 26.

4. Ibid., 19–20.

5. Bernard DeVoto, *Across the Wide Missouri*, 388.

6. Dale L. Morgan, ed., *The West of William H. Ashley*, xlvi–xlvii.

7. Ibid., 106.

8. T. D. Bonner, ed., *The Life and Adventures of James P. Beckwourth*, 53.

9. Morgan, ed., *The West of Ashley*, 106.

10. Ibid.

11. Harrison Clifford Dale, ed., *The Ashley–Smith Explorations and the Discovery of a Central Route to the Pacific 1822–1829*, 141.

12. J. W. Powell, *Exploration of the Colorado River and Its Canyons*, 158. The inscription had weathered so much by the time the Powell crew saw it that the date was hard to read. According to an old-time mountaineer who Powell had talked to, Ashley and his crew were wrecked, with only Ashley and one other surviving the disaster. These two climbed the canyon wall and made their way to Salt Lake City, where the Mormons gave them food and clothing and put them to work on the foundations of the Temple. Later, Ashley was supposed to have returned and settled in the area, thus giving Ashley Valley its name. This story has elements of the truth in it, but it also sounds like what happened to some of the men with William Manly. There seems to be another story mixed in with this tale, however. Could this be some other party who tried to make their way down the river? Others did indeed try the river route after Ashley and before Major Powell explored the canyons in 1869. These later river travelers, with one exception, have unfortunately left no records.

13. Morgan, *Jedediah Smith*, 165.

14. Dale, ed., *The Ashley–Smith Explorations*, 142–43.

15. Ibid., 144–45.

16. Bonner, ed., *James P. Beckwourth*, 59–60. No one has ever really figured out just where the "Green River Suck" was located. Ralf Woolley thought it must be just where the river entered Flaming Gorge. The legend was current in Green River, Wyoming, into the twentieth century.

17. Morgan, ed., *The West of Ashley*, 281.

18. Glade Ross, personal communication.

19. LeRoy R. Hafen, ed., *The Mountain Men and the Fur Trade of the Far West*, 177–90.

20. Frances Fuller Victor, *The River of the West*, 260.

21. LeRoy R. Hafen, "Fort Davy Crockett, Its Fur Men and Visitors," *Colorado Magazine* 29 (1952):14.

22. Bil Gilbert, *Westering Man*, 172. Walker was very interested in the canyons of the Green and the Colorado and tried on several occasions to organize an expedition to explore the rivers by boat.

23. Thomas Jefferson Farnham, *Travels in the Great Western Prairies*, 111.

24. Hafen, "Fort Davy Crockett," 15–16.

25. U.S. Congress, Senate, *Report of the Exploring Expedition*, 279.

CHAPTER THREE

1. U.S. Congress, Senate, *Report of the Exploring Expedition*, 129–30.

2. William Lewis Manly, *Death Valley in '49*, 1–53. The party consisted of Manly, John Rodgers, M. S. McMahon, Charles and Joseph Hazelbrig, Alfred Walton, and Richard Field. Frank F. Latta, *Death Valley 49'ers*, 44–49.

3. Manly, *Death Valley*, 60.

4. Ibid., 61.

5. Ibid., 69–70.

6. Ibid., 69.

7. Ibid., 71–72.

8. Ibid., 73.

9. Ibid., 73–74.

10. Ibid., 75.

11. Ibid., 79–80. Powell noted the abandoned boat and other equipment when he ran Lodore in 1869, but assumed that the gear was left by Manly's party. Manly wrote his account of the river trip from memory, nearly fifty years later.

12. Ibid., 85–86.

13. Ibid., 87.

14. Howard A. Christy, "Open Hand and Mailed Fist: Mormon–Indian Relations in Utah, 1847–1852," *Utah Historical Quarterly* 46 (Summer 1978):234.

15. Manly, *Death Valley*, 88–89.

16. Ibid., 93.

17. Ibid., 94.

18. Ibid., 95–96.

19. Ibid., 396–429.

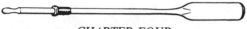

CHAPTER FOUR

1. Since it was first published by the Smithsonian Institution in 1875, Powell's book has been through many editions. Two biographies have been written about Powell and his career, *Powell of the Colorado* by William Culp Darrah, and *Beyond the Hundredth Meridian*, by Wallace Stegner. Besides these, many other books, articles, and even poems have been written about the voyages. Walt Disney Productions produced a movie version of the expeditions, *Ten Who Dared*, which rehashed the story in a rather melodramatic way, and another film version of the voyage, *Grand Canyon: The Hidden Secrets*, is shown daily in a special theater at the south rim of the Grand Canyon.

2. William Culp Darrah, "Biographical Sketches and Original Documents of the First Powell Expedition of 1869," *Utah Historical Quarterly* 15 (1947):10.

3. Ibid.

4. Robert Brewster Stanton, *Colorado River Controversies*, 97–132. Stanton is an excellent source for little-known details about the Colorado River, and history owes him a debt for collecting what would otherwise have been lost. It must be remembered, however, that while he admired Major Powell for his initial exploration and his other accomplishments, he felt strongly that the Major's report was inaccurate and moreover, unfair to those who had accompanied him.

5. Stegner, *Beyond the Hundredth Meridian,* 151–52. In this section, Stegner gives a good explanation of the reasons why Powell wrote a romanticized version of the two river journeys.

6. Darrah, "Biographical Sketches," 30.

7. Stegner, *Beyond the Hundredth Meridian*, 9–17.

8. Ibid., 56–60. Sumner claimed that the idea of exploring the canyons was originally his. See Stanton, *Controversies*, 169–70.

9. Stanton, *Controversies*, 173.

10. J. W. Powell, *The Exploration of the Colorado River and Its Canyons*, 119.

11. Stanton, *Controversies*, 174.

12. Ibid., 145. Hawkins goes on to say, "When the Major got his mail at the Virgin, he heard that the young man had gone home and said our grub did not suit him, and that he thought the Major had a rough crowd with him."

13. O. "Dock" Marston, "The Lost Journal of John Colton Sumner," *Utah Historical Quarterly* 37 (Spring 1969):175.

14. Ibid.

15. Ibid.

16. Ibid.

17. As described in Chapter One, almost all of the names for canyons, rapids, and other topographical features on the Green River come from Powell's two crews.

18. Darrah, "Biographical Sketches," 32.

19. Marston, "John Colton Sumner," 178.

20. Darrah, "Biographical Sketches," 34–35.

21. Ibid., 38.

22. Marston, "John Colton Sumner," 179. Ironically, some of these must have been Colorado River Squawfish, which are now an endangered species and highly prized by wildlife biologists.

23. Stegner, *Beyond the Hundredth Meridian*, 57.

24. Frederick S. Dellenbaugh, *A Canyon Voyage*, 25. In light of the later successful designs of Nathaniel Galloway, Dellenbaugh's comment about the "flat-bottomed and inadequate" boats is interesting.

25. The oxen probably belonged to the Mormons who kept the oxen they used for the migrations to the Salt Lake Valley in Browns Park.

26. Marston, "John Colton Sumner," 179–80.

27. Darrah, "Biographical Sketches," 96–97.

28. Powell, *Exploration of the Colorado*, 156.

29. Stanton, *Controversies*, 147, 177.

30. Darrah, "Biographical Sketches," 37.

31. Wallace Stegner, ed., *This Is Dinosaur*, 61.

32. Darrah, "Biographical Sketches," 40.

33. Ann Zwinger, *Run, River, Run*, 155.

34. Marston, "John Colton Sumner," 184.

35. Ibid., 186.

36. Darrah, "Biographical Sketches," 41.

37. Ibid., 103–4.

38. Marston, "John Colton Sumner," 186.

39. Ibid.

40. Darrah, "Biographical Sketches," 44.

41. Ibid., 108.

42. "Vernal Memorial Park Rendezvous for Many Great River Runners," *The Vernal Express*, 22 July 1973.

CHAPTER FIVE

1. At the bottom of the Grand Canyon, at a rapid they later named Separation Rapid (reputed to be one of the worst on the river and now under Lake Mead), O. G. Howland, Seneca Howland, and Bill Dunn decided to quit the party and take their chances on a climb to the rim of the canyon. There they would strike out overland and try to reach the Mormon settlement of Kanab. Powell tried to dissuade them from leaving, and they tried to convince him to abandon the river. Neither was successful. The two Howlands and Dunn succeeded in reaching the north rim of the Grand Canyon, only to be set upon and murdered by a band of Shivwits Indians. The Shivwits were seeking revenge for the molestation and murder of one of their women by some prospectors. Powell's men were, unhappily, the first white men they came across. Powell only learned of their fate when he visited the Shivwits with Jacob Hamblin in 1871.

2. Wallace Stegner, *Beyond the Hundredth Meridian*, 113.

3. Ibid., 114.

4. Frederick S. Dellenbaugh, *Romance of the Colorado River*, 244. Except for the Major, however, none of the crew wore their life preservers.

5. William Culp Darrah, "Major Powell Prepares for a Second Expedition," *Utah Historical Quarterly* 15 (1947):150-51. For the standard biography of Jacob Hamblin, see *Jacob Hamblin, Mormon Apostle to the Indians*, by Juanita Brooks. A biography of Dodds, who played an equally important role in the Uinta Basin, has yet to be written. Sources on him are limited to a tape of his youngest son, Joe Dodds, recorded by Mike Brown in 1978, and *Builders of Uintah*, the centennial history of the Uinta Basin put out by the Daughters of Utah Pioneers in 1947.

6. Stegner, *Beyond the Hundredth Meridian*, 124-25. The *Utah Historical Quarterly*, volumes 15-17, which were published in 1947-49, contain excellent short biographical sketches of all the crew members on both of Powell's voyages. Virtually every historian who has studied both voyages has commented on the different composition of the two crews.

7. William Culp Darrah, *Powell of the Colorado*, 163-64.

8. E. O. Beaman, "The Cañon of the Colorado, and the Moquis Pueblos," *Appleton's Journal* 11 (18 April 1874):5.

9. Herbert E. Gregory, ed., "Diary of Almon Harris Thompson," *Utah Historical Quarterly* 7 (January, April, July 1939):14.

10. Don D. Fowler, ed., *Photographed All the Best Scenery*, 30.

11. Darrah, *Powell of the Colorado*, 167.

12. Fowler, ed., *Photographed All the Best Scenery*, 26; Frederick S. Dellenbaugh, *A Canyon Voyage*, 31.

13. Other sources attribute the change to Elizabeth Bassett, who settled in Browns Park with her family in the 1870s. According to this version, when they entered the park she exclaimed: "No place as lovely as this ever should have been called a 'hole.' It's more like a park . . . Brown's Park!" John Rolfe Burroughs, *Where the Old West Stayed Young*, 41.

14. William Culp Darrah, ed., "Journal of Stephen Vandiver Jones," *Utah Historical Quarterly* 16-17 (1948-49):39.

15. Fowler, Ed., *Photographed All the Best Scenery*, 35.

16. Beaman, "Cañon of the Colorado," 16.

17. Charles Kelly, ed., "Journal of W. C. Powell," *Utah Historical Quarterly* 16-17 (1948-49):274.

18. Darrah, ed., "John F. Steward," 195. Bishop and Jones, who were both very religious, were quite offended by this choice of names and preferred Thompson's suggestion, Boulder Falls.

19. Fowler, ed., *Photographed All the Best Scenery*, 37.

20. Gregory, ed., "Almon Harris Thompson," 22.

21. Dellenbaugh, *A Canyon Voyage*, 51. I climbed along the side of Lodore Canyon in the summer of 1983 to the same spot where Steward and Clem took their midnight swim. A dike of hard, angular limestone forms a gate across the river, and the whirlpool below looks dangerous even in full daylight.

22. Sue Watson, originally a Ruple of Island Park, has said Jones Hole was named for a local cowhand who hid out there one winter, mistakenly believing that he had killed a man in a fight.

23. Dellenbaugh, *A Canyon Voyage*, 55.

24. Fowler, ed., *Photographed All the Best Scenery*, 47.

25. Beaman, "Cañon of the Colorado," 22.

26. Gregory, ed., "Almon Harris Thompson," 26–27.

27. The members of the second expedition seemed reluctant to discuss the journey except of course for Dellenbaugh. When questioned about the inaccuracies in Powell's report by Robert Brewster Stanton, Prof Thompson declined any comment, much to Stanton's frustration. Dellenbaugh remained staunchy loyal to Powell all his life, his admiration bordering on adulation. Powell seemed to arouse strong emotions in all who knew him. Stanton and Stone both delighted in proving him wrong; in Stanton's case it was almost a higher calling. There was little middle ground where Powell was concerned.

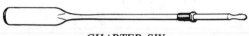

CHAPTER SIX

1. Morgan, *Great Salt Lake*, 325.

2. U.S. Department of the Interior, Bureau of Land Management, *John Jarvie of Brown's Park*, 33, 54–55.

3. C. Gregory Crampton Papers, "Boating on the Upper Colorado: A History of the Navigational Use of the Green, Colorado, and San Juan Rivers and Their Major Tributaries," 57.

4. Lewis R. Freeman, *The Colorado River: Yesterday, Today, and Tomorrow*, 327.

5. Wallace Stegner, ed., *This is Dinosaur*, 61.

6. Ibid., 63.

7. Don Hatch, interview.

8. In later years Galloway often stopped to visit with Preston Nutter, his friend and sometime employer, who moved into the Nine Mile Canyon area in 1902. Stone and Galloway met Nutter when they passed the mouth of Nine Mile Creek in 1909. Preston Nutter Corporation Papers, Letter, 11 June 1911, Nathaniel Galloway to Preston Nutter.

9. "Through the Grand Canyon of the Colorado: Adventures by Nathan Galloway," *The Vernal Express*, 7 July 1898–14 July 1898.

10. Otis "Dock" Marston, "River Runners—Fast-Water Navigation," *Utah Historical Quarterly* 28 (July 1960):292–93.

11. David Lavender, *River Runners of the Grand Canyon*, 40. Stone suggested some changes, which were incorporated into the design. The resulting craft was thereafter known as the "Galloway–Stone boat."

12. Julius F. Stone, *Canyon Country: The Romance of a Drop of Water and a Grain of Sand*, 46.

13. Ibid., 50.

14. U.S. Department of the Interior, Bureau of Land Management, *John Jarvie*, 79–83.

15. Stone, *Canyon Country*, 54. Stone floated the river with Powell's report in hand, checking up on him as he went.

16. Ibid., 55.

17. Ibid.

18. Ibid., 56.

19. Ibid., 57.

20. The dinosaur quarry is still in operation at this writing (1986).

21. "People and Incidents," *The Vernal Express*, 27 December 1913; "Noted Trapper and Guide is No More," *The Richfield Reaper*, 3 January 1914.

22. E. L. Kolb, *Through the Grand Canyon from Wyoming to Mexico*, 11–91.

23. Ibid., 20.

24. Ibid., 44.

25. Ibid., 51.

26. Ibid., 59.

27. Ibid., 70.

28. "Echo Park History," Uintah County Historical Society.

29. Frank Sarles, "History of Dinosaur National Monument," 1964, Headquarters Library Dinosaur National Monument, 70–74.

30. Ibid., 74.

31. Ralph Chew, interview.

32. Kolb, *Through the Grand Canyon*, 75.

33. Chew interview.

34. Kolb, *Through the Grand Canyon*, 76–77.

35. Ellsworth Kolb and Emery Kolb, "Experiences in the Grand Canyon," *National Geographic* 26 (August 1914): 99–184.

CHAPTER SEVEN

1. Otis "Dock" Marston, "River Runners—Fast-Water Navigation," *Utah Historical Quarterly* 28 (July 1960): 292.

2. Gregory C. Crampton, Papers, 32; Ila Cowan, *Jensen, Utah: Where Is It? Who Are Its People?* Not surprisingly, the town of Jensen was named after Jens's father, Lars. Jens ran the Green about twelve years later, and in 1940 ran the Yampa in an open boat with a load of mining machinery. He was fifty-nine years old at the time.

3. "Steamboat Being Built," *Green River Star*, 1 May 1908; "The Steamboat a Success," *Green River Star*, 17 July 1908.

4. "Down the Colorado," *Green River Star*, 18 June 1909; "Voyagers Return But Leave Boat," *Green River Star*, 25 June 1909.

5. F. LeMoyne Page, "My Trip Down the Green River," 1926.

6. "Diary of H. Elwyn Blake, Jr.,'' 1926.

7. In the summer of 1983, a passenger on a commercial river trip drowned when the raft he was riding in was pinned against a rock in Triplet Falls.

8. "Diary of Blake," 5–6.

9. Page, "My Trip," 10–11.

10. The boat was recovered the next year by Parley Galloway.

11. *Denver Post*, August 17–September 5, 1928.

12. "Post's Yampa Cañon Expedition Safe," *Denver Post*, 29 August 1928.

13. Wallace Stegner, ed., *This Is Dinosaur*, 67.

14. Laura Evans and Buzz Belknap, *Dinosaur River Guide*, 31.

15. Robert Ormand Case, "He Shot the Colorado Alone," *Saturday Evening Post* 210 (26 February 1938):8.

16. "Diary of 'Buzz' Holmstrom's Trip Down the Colorado—Oct. 4–Nov. 20—1937."

17. Ann Zwinger, *Run, River, Run*, 160–61.

18. Buzz Holmstrom, Papers, 5.

19. Ibid., 6–7.

20. "French Trio Leave on Perilous Trip Down Green River," *The Vernal Express*, 15 September 1938.

21. Ibid.

22. Stegner, ed., *This Is Dinosaur*, 68; W. Stewart Gardiner, interview; Hatch interview.

23. "Three Expeditions Now on Trips Down the Green River," *The Vernal Express*, 22 September 1938.

24. Roy DeSpain, interview. Roy DeSpain reported that Bernard filled a pie tin with sand and placed birthday candles in it, a European tradition. When he came from around a boulder with the "cake" and all began singing, Genevieve burst into tears. Four of the fish and game party painted their names on the eastern wall, just at the foot of Triplet Falls, where they can still be seen.

25. "French Trio Reach Split Mt. on Trip to Boulder," *The Vernal Express*, 29 September 1938; "Frenchmen Rig Boats with Motor," *The Vernal Express*, 6 October 1938.

26. Wes Eddington, who it will be remembered was a member of the wildlife survey party, was so taken by the folding kayaks used by the DeColmonts and DeSeyne that he ordered one for himself, and in 1940 took it on an autumn trip through Desolation Canyon with Roy DeSpain. DeSpain Interview.

27. Gardiner interview.

28. "Lone Adventurer Making Trip Down Colorado," *The Vernal Express*, 14 September 1939; "Boatman Arrives at Jensen on Trip to Boulder," *The Vernal Express*, 28 September 1939.

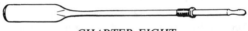

CHAPTER EIGHT

1. *Builders of Uintah*, 247. Ratliff actually spent a considerable part of his career as an engineer in and around the canyons of the upper Green and Yampa. Besides the 1901 trip, he was on the river as a surveyor in 1910, 1915, 1919 (with Earl Douglass), and 1923. From 1918-20 he lived at Hell's Canyon on the upper Yampa. Upper Colorado River Commission, *Official Record*, vol. 2, 1950, 119.

2. U.S. Department of the Interior, Reclamation Service, *Eighth Annual Report of the Reclamation Service, 1908-1909*, 57.

3. E. L. Kolb, *Through the Grand Canyon from Wyoming to Mexico*, 49.

4. U.S. Department of the Interior, Reclamation Service, *Eighth Annual Report*, 53.

5. Otis "Dock" Marston, "River Runners—Fast-Water Navigation," *Utah Historical Quarterly* 28 (July 1960):293.

6. "Report on Reconnaissance Investigation of the Green River, from Green River, Wyoming, to Green River, Utah," Utah Power and Light Co., 1 October 1917, photocopy, 5.

7. U.S. Department of the Interior, Geological Survey, *The Green River and Its Utilization*, 39-50; "Power Possibilities of the Green River between Green River, Wyoming and Green River, Utah," Utah Power and Light Co., 1 March 1923, photocopy. The engineer in charge was K. W. Trimble. Other personnel, besides Woolley, were J. B. Reeside, Jr., geologist; H. L. Stoner, representing Utah Power and Light; and John Clogston, cook.

8. Ibid., 38.

9. Ibid., 42.

10. Ibid.

11. Ibid., 46.

12. Ibid., 47.

13. Susan Mae Neel, "Utah and the Echo Park Dam Controversy," 2.

14. Ibid.

15. *Builders of Uintah*, 276.

16. "The Mountain West is Counting on the Republican Party to Back Ike and the Party in the Fight for the Colorado River Storage Project."

17. "Echo Park Dam Will Create a Playground for Millions."

18. "This Is The Echo Park Country as It Looks Today . . . Tomorrow's Playground for Millions of Americans."

19. Ibid.

20. Ibid.

21. Ibid.

22. "Echo Park Dam."

23. "New Evidence Proves Echo Park Legally Reserved for Dam Site," *Colorado River News*.

24. U.S. *Statutes at Large*, vol. 39, Stat. 535, "P.L. 64-235," 24 August 1916.

25. U.S. Department of the Interior, National Park Service, *A Survey of the Recreational Resources of the Colorado River Basin*, 196-97.

26. Philip L. Fradkin, *A River No More: The Colorado River and the West*, 192-97.

27. Neel, "Utah and Echo Park," 65-68.

28. Fradkin, *A River No More*, 192-97.

29. Senate Committee, *Storage Project*, 327.

30. U.S. *Statutes at Large* 70 Stat. 105, "P.L. 84-485," 11 April 1956. The House vote was 256 for, 136 against. The Senate vote was 58 for, 23 against. It must be noted that many versions of the bill were introduced, modified, and rejected before the final legislation was passed. The Colorado River Storage Project has a very complicated legislative history.

31. Neel, "Utah and Echo Park," 105-11.

32. Ibid., 117.

33. Indeed, many residents of the Uinta Basin refuse to even discuss the dam, although mention of it will still produce an argument in the cafes in Vernal and Roosevelt and the other small towns to this day.

34. Jim McBrayer, River Ranger, Dinosaur National Monument, Letter to author, 10 April 1984.

35. U.S. Department of the Interior, Bureau of Reclamation, *Technical Record of Design and Construction: Flaming Gorge Dam and Power Plant*, 510.

36. Ibid., 10.

37. Ibid., 295. 115 men died during the construction of Boulder Dam in the 1930s.

38. Ibid., 8. The amount of power produced by the three generators at Flaming Gorge Dam, 108,000 kilowatts, would power a city of about 50,000.

39. Dick Dunham and Vivian Dunham, *Flaming Gorge Country: The Story of Daggett County, Utah*, 337; William M. Purdy, interview. Purdy was a schoolteacher in Manila, Utah, at the time the dam was built. Charlie Crouse is a legend in Browns Park. He was a lover of fine horses, and story has it that he supplied the outlaw gangs with good mounts. He was also known for his quick temper and towering rages. For more on him, see John Rolfe Burroughs, *Where the Old West Stayed Young*.

40. Ibid., 335.

41. "Who Wants to Name a Lake?" *Deseret News*, 2 February 1963; "Keep Name the Same," *Deseret News*, 7 March 1963.

42. "Good Place to Save," *Deseret News*, 19 July 1967; "Pool Gorge Efforts," *Deseret News*, 30 March 1968.

43. John Cross, interview.

44. "Chilly Water Slows Fishing," *Salt Lake Tribune*, 27 August 1972; "Unusual Device Placed at Gorge," *Deseret News*, 9 November 1977; "Project Completion Slated Today at Flaming Gorge," *Deseret News*, 23 May 1978. The project cost an estimated $5 million.

CHAPTER NINE

1. Cort Conley, conversation.

2. Don Hatch, interview.

3. Frank Swain, interview.

4. Ibid.

5. Wallace Stegner, ed., *This Is Dinosaur*, 67.

6. Hatch interview.

7. Ibid.

8. "Nevills and Loper River Parties Visit Vernal," *The Vernal Express*, 4 July 1940.

9. Ibid., 1; Don Harris, telephone conversation.

10. C. Gregory Crampton Papers, 46.

11. *"Tales from the High Country: Stories from Uintah County, Utah,"* 41. Crampton Papers, 64, names Jim Orr as the man who accompanied Bus Hatch. Cross Mountain Gorge was not sucessfully run by a raft until 1974 by a group of commercial boatmen from Adventure Bound, Inc.

12. John Cross, interview.

13. Hatch interview.

14. "Five Women Will Make Trip with River Boat Party," *Green River Star*, 16 June 1949; P. T. Reilly, letter to author, 11 December 1985.

15. Dr. Gary Topping, "Harry Aleson and the Place No One Knew," *Utah Historical Quarterly* 52 (Spring 1984):173.

16. Harry Aleson Papers, "Notes on Green River Trip, 1951," 5.

17. Ibid., 6.

18. Cross interview.

19. Ted Woolley, Utah Division of Parks and Recreation, telephone conversation.

20. Cross interview.

21. The U.S. Coast Guard relinquished responsibility for regulating river runners in 1984. It is now controlled by the state of Utah.

22. Dee Holladay, personal communication.

23. Ibid.

24. Crampton Papers, 47; Reilly, letter, December 1985.

25. Richard Schreyer et al., "The Dinosaur National Monument Whitewater River Recreation Study."

26. Leslie Jones, "Maps and Profiles of the Green River from Green River City, Wyoming to Green River City, Utah, through Flaming Gorge, Horseshoe, Red, Swallow, Lodore, Whirlpool, Split Mountain, Desolation, and Grey Canyons."

27. Cid Ricketts Sumner, *Traveler in the Wilderness*.

28. Randall Henderson, "Boat Trip in the Canyon Lodore," *The Desert Magazine* 19 (July 1956):4–9.

29. *WAMOC Rambler*, July 1957.

30. Cal Giddings, who was on the trip, remembers that one of the men in his boat was a telephone lineman. He threw the rope to the hapless swimmer with such accuracy that it fell right into his hand. Otherwise, the man probably would have drowned.

31. U.S. Department of the Interior, National Park Service, Dinosaur National Monument, *Proposed River Management Plan: Dinosaur National Monument Colorado-Utah*.

32. Holladay conversation.

33. "On the Green: Double Trouble at Disaster Falls," *Deseret News*, 27 May 1984.

Bibliography

Abbey, Edward. *Desert Solitaire: A Season in the Wilderness*. New York: Ballantine Books, 1968.

Aleson, Harry. Papers. Utah State Historical Society, Salt Lake City.

Bacdayan and R. S. Whaley. *Secondary Economic Impact from Water Resources Development: A Case Study of Flaming Gorge Reservoir*. Utah Resources Series 50. Logan, Utah: Utah Agricultural Experiment Station, Utah State University, November 1969.

Bailey, Earl Gordon, and Herschel C. Smith. "An Economic Study of the Storage and Power Possibilities at Flaming Gorge." Bachelor's thesis, University of Utah, 1929.

Baker, Pearl. *Trail on the Water*. Boulder, Co.: Pruett Publishing Co., n.d.

Beaman, E. O. "The Cañon of the Colorado, and the Moquis Pueblos." *Appleton's Journal* 11 (18 April 1874):1–24.

Berry, Don. *A Majority of Scoundrels: An Informal History of the Rocky Mountain Fur Company*. New York: Harper and Row, 1961.

Bingham, Jay R. "Reclamation and the Colorado." *Utah Historical Quarterly* 28 (July 1960): 233–49.

Bolton, Herbert E. "Pageant in the Wilderness: the Story of the Escalante Expedition to the Interior Basin, 1776, Including the Diary and Itinerary of Father Escalante, Translated and Annotated." *Utah Historical Quarterly* 18 (1950).

Bonner, T. D. *The Life and Adventures of James P. Beckwourth*. New York: Alfred A. Knopf, 1931.

Breck, Vivian. *Whitewater*. Garden City, N.Y.: Doubleday, 1959.

Breed, Jack. "Shooting Rapids in Dinosaur Country." *National Geographic* 105 (March 1954):363–90.

Briggs, Walter. *Without Noise of Arms*. Flagstaff, Az.: Northland Press, 1976.

Brooks, Juanita. *Jacob Hamblin, Mormon Apostle to the Indians*. Salt Lake City: Howe Brothers, 1980.

Brower, David R. "Dinosaurs, Parks and Dams." *The Pacific Spectator* 8 (Spring 1954):151–66.

Builders of Uintah: A Centennial History of Uintah County 1872 to 1947. Arranged and published by Daughters of the Utah Pioneers of Uintah County, Utah. Springville, Utah: Art City Publishing Co., 1947.

Burg, Amos. Papers. Utah State Historical Society, Salt Lake City.

Burroughs, John Rolfe. *Where the Old West Stayed Young*. New York: Bonanza Books, 1962.

Burton, Richard F. *The City of the Saints and Across the Rocky Mountains to California*. New York: Alfred A. Knopf, 1963.

Butcher, Devereux, "Stop the Dinosaur Power Grab." *National Parks Magazine* 24 (Apr.–June 1950):61–65.

_____. "This Is Dinosaur." *National Parks Magazine* 24 (October–December 1950):123–37.

Case, Robert Ormond. "He Shot the Colorado Alone." *Saturday Evening Post* 210 (26 February 1938).

Chamberlin, Ralph V. "Francis Marion Bishop (1843–1943)." *Utah Historical Quarterly* 15 (1947):155–58.

Chew, Ralph. Interview by Roy Webb, 12 January 1978. Tape recording, Vernal District Office, Bureau of Land Management, Vernal, Utah.

Christy, Howard A. "Open Hand and Mailed Fist: Mormon–Indian Relations in Utah, 1847–52." *Utah Historical Quarterly* 46 (Summer 1978):216–35.

Cline, Gloria Griffen. *Exploring the Great Basin*. Norman: University of Oklahoma Press, 1963.

Colton, Hugh. Interview by Michael W. Brown, 18 December 1978. Tape recording, Uintah County Library, Vernal, Utah.

Conley, Cort. Conversation with author, March 1984, July 1985.

Cowan, Ila W. *Jensen, Utah: Where Is It? Who Are Its People?* Provo, Utah: Community Press, 1979.

Crampton, C. Gregory. "The Discovery of the Green River." *Utah Historical Quarterly* 20 (October 1952):299–312.

_____. "Humboldt's Utah, 1811." *Utah Historical Quarterly* 26 (July 1958):269–81.

_____. *Standing Up Country: The Canyon Lands of Utah and Arizona*. Salt Lake City: Gibbs M. Smith Inc., Peregrine Smith Books, 1983.

_____. Papers. University of Utah Marriott Library, Salt Lake City.

Cross, John. Interview by Roy Webb, 12 March 1984. Tape recording, University of Utah Marriott Library, Salt Lake City.

Cutter, Robert K. "Hetch Hetchy—Once is too Often," *Sierra Club Bulletin*. June 1954.

Dale, Harrison Clifford, ed. *The Ashley–Smith Explorations and the Discovery of a Central Route to the Pacific 1822–1829*. Rev. ed. Glendale, Calif.: Arthur H. Clarke Co., 1941.

Darrah, William Culp. "Biographical Sketches and Original Documents of the First Powell Expedition of 1869." *Utah Historical Quarterly* 15 (1947):9–148.

_____. "Major Powell Prepares for a Second Expedition." *Utah Historical Quarterly* 15 (1947):149–53.

_____. *Powell of the Colorado*. Princeton, N.J.: Princeton University Press, 1951.

_____. ed. "Journal of John F. Steward." *Utah Historical Quarterly* 16–17 (1948–49):181–251.

Day, Kent C., and David S. Dibble with addenda by David S. Pendergast and Kent C. Day. *Archeological Survey of the Flaming Gorge Reservoir Area, Wyoming–Utah*. Anthropological Papers, No. 65. Salt Lake City: University of Utah Press, 1963.

DeColmont, Bernard, et al. *Trois Francais en Kayak sur le Colorado: Voyage sur le Green River et le Colorado*. Paris: (n.p.), 1939.

DeColmont, Bernard. "Une Expédition Française sur le Colorado." *L'Illustration*, No. 5017. 29 April 1939.

Dellenbaugh, Frederick S. *A Canyon Voyage: The Narrative of the Second Powell Expedition Down the Green & Colorado River from Wyoming, and the Explorations on Land, in the Years 1871 and 1872*. New Haven, Conn.: Yale University Press, 1962.

_____. "The Canyon of Lodore." *Colorado Magazine* 7, no. 5 (September 1930):195–201.

_____. *The Romance of the Colorado River*. New York: G. P. Putnam's Sons, 1902.

Denver Post.

Deseret News.

DeSeyne, Antoine. Journal 28 August–9 November 1938. Photocopy.

DeSpain, Roy. Interview by Roy Webb, 20 April 1985. Tape recording, University of Utah Marriott Library, Salt Lake City.

DeVoto, Bernard. *Across the Wide Missouri*. Boston: Houghton, Mifflin, 1947.

"Diary of 'Buzz' Holmstrom's Trip Down the Colorado—Oct. 4–Nov. 20—1937," 1937. Holmstrom Papers, MSS MIC 1389. Utah State Historical Society, Salt Lake City.

"Diary of H. Elwyn Blake, Jr.," 1926. Utah State Historical Society, Salt Lake City. Photocopy.

Dunham, Dick, and Vivian Dunham. *Flaming Gorge Country: The Story of Daggett County*. Denver: Eastwood Printing and Publishing, 1977.

"Echo Park Dam Will Create a Playground for Millions." Grand Junction Colorado: Upper Colorado River Grass Roots, Inc., n.d. Brochure.

"Echo Park History." Uintah County Historical Society, July 1978. Tape recording, Vernal, Utah, Uintah County Library. Sound Cassette.

Evans, Laura, and Buzz Belknap. *Dinosaur River Guide*. Boulder City, Nev.: Westwater Books, 1973.

Farnham, Thomas Jefferson. *Travels in the Great Western Prairies, Anatuac and Rocky Mountains and in the Oregon Territory*. Poughkeepsie, N.Y.: Killey and Lossing Printers, 1841.

Fowler, Don D., and Catherine S. Fowler. "John Wesley Powell's Journal: Colorado River Exploration 1871–1872." *Smithsonian Journal of History* 3 (Summer 1968):1–44.

Fowler, Don D., ed. *"Photographed All the Best Scenery": Jack Hillers's Diary of the Powell Expeditions, 1871–1875*. Salt Lake City: University of Utah Press, 1972.

Fradkin, Philip L. *A River No More: The Colorado River and the West*. New York: Alfred A. Knopf, 1981.

Frazier, Russell G. Papers. Utah State Historical Society, Salt Lake City.

Freeman, Lewis R. *The Colorado River: Yesterday, Today, and Tomorrow*. New York: Dodd, Mead and Co., 1923.

_____. *Down the Grand Canyon*. New York: Dodd, Mead and Co., 1924.

Gardiner, W. Stewart. Interview by Roy Webb, 3 July 1984. Tape recording, University of Utah Marriott Library, Salt Lake City.

——————. "A Trip Down the Green River: From Henry's Fork to Jensen, Utah; October 23rd to October 31st 1938." Photocopy.

——————. "River Rocks and Rapids." Photocopy.

Giddings, Cal. Interview by Roy Webb, 3 July 1984. Tape recording. University of Utah Marriott Library, Salt Lake City.

Gilbert, Bil. *Westering Man: The Life of Joseph Walker, Master of the Frontier.* New York: Atheneum, 1983.

Goetzmann, William H. *Army Exploration in the American West 1803–1863.* New Haven, Conn.: Yale University Press, 1959.

Goldwater, Barry M. *An Odyssey of the Green and Colorado Rivers: The Intimate Journal of Three Boats and Nine People on a Trip Down Two Rivers.* Phoenix: 1941.

Gowans, Fred R. *Rocky Mountain Rendezvous.* Provo, Utah: Brigham Young University Press, 1976.

Graf, William L. "The Wild Canyon of Lodore." *National Parks and Conservation Magazine* (February 1979):5–9.

Green River and Flaming Gorge Reservoir: Post-Impoundment Investigations, 1966. A Joint Report of the Utah State Division of Fish and Game, Wyoming Game and Fish Commission. Progress Report no. 4.

Green River Star.

Gregory, Herbert E., ed. "Diary of Almon Harris Thompson." *Utah Historical Quarterly* 7 (January, April, July, 1939):11–40.

——————. "Journal of Stephen Vandiver Jones." *Utah Historical Quarterly* 16–17 (1948–49):19–174.

Gunnerson, James H. *An Archeological Survey of the Fremont Area.* Anthropological Papers, No. 28. Salt Lake City: University of Utah Press, 1957.

Hafen, LeRoy R. "Fort Davy Crockett, its Fur Men and Visitors," *Colorado Magazine* 29 (1952).

Hafen, LeRoy R., and Ann W. Hafen. *Old Spanish Trail Santa Fe to Los Angeles with Extracts from Contemporary Records and Including Diaries of Antonio Armijo and Orville Pratt.* Glendale, Calif.: Arthur H. Clark, 1954.

Hafen, LeRoy R., and Carl Coke Rister. *Western America: The Exploration, Settlement, and Development of the Region Beyond the Mississippi.* 2nd ed. Englewood Cliffs, N.J.: Prentice-Hall, 1950.

——————, ed. *The Mountain Men and the Fur Trade of the Far West: Biographical Sketches of the Participants by Scholars of the Subject and with Introductions by the Editor.* Vol. 7. Glendale, Calif.: Arthur H. Clark Co., 1969.

Harris, Don. Telephone conversation with Roy Webb, 9 September 1984.

Hatch, Don. Interview by Roy Webb, 10 March 1984. Tape recording, University of Utah Marriott Library, Salt Lake City.

Henderson, Randall. "Boat Trip in the Canyon of Lodore." *Desert Magazine* 19 (July 1956): 4–9.

Holladay, Dee. Conversation with Roy Webb, 15 August 1984.

Holmstrom, Buzz. Papers. Utah State Historical Society, Salt Lake City.

Hunter, Zena M. *The Story of the Colorado River*. Garden City, N.Y.: Doubleday, 1960.

Inventory of the County Archives of Utah: No. 24 Uintah County (Vernal). Prepared by the Utah Historical Records Survey, Division of Professional and Service Projects, Works Projects Administration, Utah State Historical Society, sponsor. Ogden, Utah: Utah Historical Records Survey, November 1940.

Jennings, Jesse D. *Prehistory of North America*. 2nd ed. New York: McGraw–Hill, 1974.

Jones, Leslie. Interview by Roy Webb, 1 September 1985. Tape recording, University of Utah Marriott Library, Salt Lake City.

——————. "Maps and Profiles of the Green River from Green River City, Wyoming, to Green River City, Utah, through Flaming Gorge, Horseshoe, Red, Swallow, Lodore, Whirlpool, Split Mountain, Desolation and Grey Canyons." Heber City, Utah: Western Whitewater, 1955.

Kelly, Charles. Papers. University of Utah Marriott Library, Salt Lake City.

——————. "The Canyon of Lodore–Yampa River Reconnaissance of 1936." *Trail and Timberline* 219 (January 1937).

——————. "The Mysterious D. Julien." *Utah Historical Quarterly* 6 (July 1933):83–88.

——————, ed. "Capt. Francis Marion Bishop's Journal." *Utah Historical Quarterly* 15 (1947):159–238.

——————. ed. "Journal of W. C. Powell." *Utah Historical Quarterly* 16–17 (1948–49):257–487.

Kelner, Alexis. Personal communication with Roy Webb, 20 June 1984.

Kissner, Jacob. *Fabulous Folbot Holidays*. Charleston, S.C.: Creative Holiday Guides, 1970.

Kolb, Ellsworth L. *Through the Grand Canyon from Wyoming to Mexico*. New York: Macmillan, 1941.

Kolb, Ellsworth, and Emery Kolb. "Experiences in the Grand Canyon." *National Geographic* 26 (August 1914):99–184.

Latta, Frank F. *Death Valley 49'ers*. Santa Cruz, Calif.: Bear Valley Books, 1979.

Lavender, David. *Colorado River Country*. New York: Dutton, 1982.

——————. *River Runners of the Grand Canyon*. Tucson, Az.: Grand Canyon Natural History Association and University of Arizona Press, 1985.

Lee, Katie. Interview by Roy Webb, 14 April 1984. Tape recording, University of Utah Marriott Library, Salt Lake City.

Mahoney, J. R. *Navigability of the Green River: Management of Its Waters for Resource Development*. Studies in Utah's Resources of Regional Development, Utah Public Lands Research, sponsored by Utah State Land Board and University of Utah. Salt Lake City: Bureau of Economic and Business Research, College of Business, University of Utah, October 1964.

Manly, William L. *Death Valley in '49: An Important Chapter of California Pioneer History.* 1894. New York: Wallace Hebberd, 1929.

Marston, Otis "Dock." "The Grand Canyon Boat Parade." Westerners San Diego Corral, *The Wrangler* 4 (March 1971):1–7.

——————. "The Lost Journal of John Colton Sumner." *Utah Historical Quarterly* 37 (Spring 1969):173–89.

——————. "River Runners—Fast-Water Navigation." *Utah Historical Quarterly* 28 (July 1960):291–308.

——————. Brooks Papers. Utah State Historical Society, Salt Lake City.

——————. "With Powell on the Colorado." *Westerners San Diego Corrall Brand Book* (1970).

Matlin, Leonard. *The Disney Films.* New York: Crown Publishers, 1973.

McBrayer, Jim. Letter to Roy Webb, 10 April 1984.

McCall, C. W. "Green River." *Black Bear Road.* Hollywood: M.G.M. Records, Inc., 1975. Sound recording.

Millhiser, Marlys, *Willing Hostage.* New York: G.P. Putnam's Sons, 1976.

Morgan, Dale L. *The Great Salt Lake.* 1947. Albuquerque: University of New Mexico Press, 1973.

——————. *Jedediah Smith and the Opening of the West.* Lincoln: University of Nebraska Press, 1953.

——————. ed. *The West of William H. Ashley.* Denver: Old West Publishing Co., 1964.

Moss, Frank. Papers. University of Utah Marriott Library, Salt Lake City.

"The Mountain West is Counting on the Republican Party to Back Ike and the Party in the Fight for the Colorado River Storage Project." (1952). Brochure. Sponsored by Republicans of Mountain West States.

Neel, Susan Mae. "Utah and the Echo Park Dam Controversy." Master's thesis, University of Utah, 1980.

Nevills, Norman. Edited Journal. Marston Papers. Huntington Library, San Marino, Calif.

"New Evidence Proves Echo Park Legally Reserved for Dam Site." *Colorado River News.* Grand Junction, Co.: Upper Colorado Grass Roots, Inc., n.d.

Nutter, Preston. Corporation Papers. University of Utah Marriott Library, Salt Lake City.

Oravec, Christine. "Conservationism vs. Preservationism: The 'Public Interest' in the Hetch Hetchy Controversy." *Quarterly Journal of Speech* 70 (1984):444–58.

Packard, Fred M. "Dinosaur Dams Again." *National Parks Magazine* 28 (January–March 1954):2–5.

Page, F. LeMoyne, "My Trip Down the Green River," 1926. Utah State Historical Society, Salt Lake City. Photocopy.

Powell, J. W. *The Exploration of the Colorado River and Its Canyons.* New York: Dover Publications, 1961.

"Power Possibilities of the Green River Between Green River, Wyoming, and Green River, Utah." Utah Power and Light Co., Engineering Dept., 1923. Photocopy.

Purdy, William M. Interview by Roy Webb, 28 August 1985. Tape recording, University of Utah Marriott Library, Salt Lake City.

_____. "Green River: Main Stem of the Colorado," *Utah Historical Quarterly* 28 (July 1960):250–61.

_____. *An Outline of the History of the Flaming Gorge Area.* Anthropological Papers, No. 37. Salt Lake City: University of Utah Press, 1959.

Ratliff, James H. "Ice Conditions on the Green and Yampa Rivers, Moffat County, Colorado, and Uintah County, Utah, 1901." *Official Record*, vol. 2., Transcripts of Public Hearings on the Upper Colorado River Storage Project. Upper Colorado River Commission, 1950, 87–142.

Reilly, P. T. Letter to Roy Webb, 11 December 1985.

"Report on Reconnaissance Investigation of the Green River from Green River, Wyoming to Green River, Utah." Utah Power and Light Co. October 1917. Photocopy.

Reynolds, A. K. Telephone conversation with Roy Webb, July 1985.

Ross, Glade. Personal communication with Roy Webb, July 1979.

Sarles, Frank. "History of Dinosaur National Monument." 1964. MSS in Headquarters Library, Dinosaur National Monument, Dinosaur, Colorado. Photocopy.

Schreyer, Richard, et al. *The Dinosaur National Monument Whitewater River Recreation Study.* Institute for the Study of Outdoor Recreation and Tourism, Department of Forestry and Outdoor Recreation, Utah State University, Logan, Utah, 1976.

"Sheriff Swain," *Kennescope* (November 1954):4.

Siddoway, Ralph. Interview by Michael W. Brown, 4 December 1978. Tape recording, Uintah County Library, Vernal, Utah.

Stanton, Robert Brewster. *Colorado River Controversies.* New York: Dodd, Mead and Co., 1932.

Staveley, Gaylord. *Broken Waters Sing: Rediscovering Two Great Rivers of the West.* Boston: Little, Brown and Co., 1971.

_____. Interview by Roy Webb, 13 April 1984. Tape recording, University of Utah Marriott Library, Salt Lake City.

"Steamboats Seemed a Good Idea, But Not for Long." *Pacific Power and Light Pioneer* 2 (November 1974):1–4.

Stegner, Wallace. "Battle for the Wilderness." *New Republic* (15 February 1954):13–15.

_____. *Beyond the Hundredth Meridian: John Wesley Powell and the Second Opening of the West.* Boston: Houghton, Mifflin, 1954.

_____, ed. *This Is Dinosaur: Echo Park Country and Its Magic Rivers.* New York: Alfred A. Knopf, 1955.

Stewart, George. Conversation with Roy Webb, 15 August 1981.

Stone, Julius F. *Canyon Country: The Romance of a Drop of Water and a Grain of Sand.* New York: G. P. Putnam's Sons, 1932.

Stratton, Owen, and Phillip Sirotkin. "The Echo Park Dam Controversy and
    Upper Colorado River Development." Wellesley, Mass.: Wellesley Col-
    lege, 1957. Photocopy.
Stringham, Bry. Interview by Michael W. Brown, 22 November 1978. Tape
    recording, Uintah County Library, Vernal, Utah.
Sumner, Cid Ricketts. *Travelers in the Wilderness.* New York: Harper and
    Row, 1957.
Swain, Frank. Interview by Roy Webb and Gregory C. Thompson, 2 March
    1984. Tape recording, University of Utah Marriott Library, Salt Lake City.
"Tales from the High Country: Stories from Uintah County." Collected by
    Uintah County Historical Society. Salt Lake City: Precision Text, 1982.
"This Is the Echo Park Country as It Looks Today . . . Tomorrow's Play-
    ground for Millions of Americans." Published and distributed by the Upper
    Colorado River Commission, Grand Junction, Co., n.d. Brochure.
Topping, Gary. "Harry Aleson and the Place No One Knew." *Utah Histori-
    cal Quarterly* 52 (Spring 1984):165–78.
Turville, Dennis. "The Green River: 90 Miles by Kayak." *St. George Maga-
    zine* (Summer 1984):64–69.
Tyler, S. Lyman. "Before Escalante: An Early History of the Yuta Indians
    and the Area North of New Mexico." Ph.D. diss., University of Utah,
    1951.
U.S. Congress. Senate. *Report of the Exploring Expedition to the Rocky Moun-
    tains in the Year 1842 and to Oregon and North California in the Years
    1843–44, by J. C. Frémont.* Washington, D.C.: Gales and Seaton, 1845.
————. Committee on Interior and Insular Affairs. Colorado River
    Storage Project., 84th Cong., 1st sess., 1955. Washington, D.C.: Govern-
    ment Printing Office, 1955.
U.S. Department of Agriculture. Utah and Wyoming. Ashley National For-
    est. *Flaming Gorge National Recreation Area: Final Environmental State-
    ment and Management Plan.* N.d.
U.S. Department of the Interior. Bureau of Land Management. *John Jarvie
    of Brown's Park.* By William L. Tennent. Cultural Resource Monographs
    no. 7. Salt Lake City: Bureau of Land Management, 1981.
————. Bureau of Reclamation. *The Colorado River: A Natural Men-
    ace Becomes a National Resource.* Washington, D.C.: Government Print-
    ing Office, 1946.
————. Bureau of Reclamation. *Flaming Gorge.* Washington, D.C.:
    Government Printing Office, 1979. Brochure.
————. Bureau of Reclamation. *Technical Record of Design and Con-
    struction: Flaming Gorge Dam and Power Plant, Constructed 1958–1964,
    Colorado River Storage Project, Utah.* Denver: Bureau of Reclamation,
    1968.
————. Bureau of Reclamation. Upper Colorado Region. *Colorado
    River Storage Project Information Sheet, Flaming Gorge Dam & Power
    Plant, Flaming Gorge Reservoir.* Dutch John, Utah: Flaming Gorge Field
    Division, July 1983.

_____. Geological Survey. *The Geologic Story of the Uinta Mountains.* Geological Survey Bulletin 1291. Washington, D.C.: Government Printing Office, 1969.

_____. Geological Survey. *The Green River and Its Utilization,* by Ralf R. Woolley. Water–Supply Paper 618. Washington, D.C.: Government Printing Office, 1930.

_____. National Park Service. *Exploring the American West, 1803–1879.* National Park Handbook 116. Washington, D.C.: Government Printing Office, 1982.

_____. National Park Service. *Report on the Yampa Canyon Proposed National Monument to Arno B. Cammerer.* By Roger W. Toll, Washington, D.C.: Government Printing Office, 1933.

_____. National Park Service. *Shall Dams Be Built in Dinosaur National Monument?* Excerpts from the testimony presented to the Honorable Oscar L. Chapman, Secretary of the Interior, at a public hearing held in Washington, D.C., 3 April 1950. Washington, D.C.: National Park Service, 1950.

_____. National Park Service. *A Survey of the Recreational Resources of the Colorado River Basin.* Washington, D.C.: Government Printing Office, 1950.

_____. National Park Service. *Wilderness Recommendation: Dinosaur National Monument Utah–Colorado.* Denver: Denver Service Center, August 1974.

_____. National Park Service. *Wilderness Study: Dinosaur National Monument Colorado–Utah.* Denver: Denver Service Center, January 1973.

_____. National Park Service. Dinosaur National Monument. *Proposed River Management Plan: Dinosaur National Monument Colorado–Utah.* August 1979.

_____. Reclamation Service. *Seventh Annual Report of the Reclamation Service 1907–1908.* Washington, D.C.: Government Printing Office, 1908.

_____. Reclamation Service. *Eighth Annual Report of the Reclamation Service 1908–1909.* Washington, D.C.: Government Printing Office, 1910.

U.S. Statutes at Large, vol. 39, Stat. 535, "P.L. 64–235," 25 August 1916; 70 Stat. 105, "P.L. 84–485," 11 April 1956.

Untermann, G. E. Papers. University of Utah Marriott Library, Salt Lake City.

Upper Colorado River Commission. *Official Record.* Transcripts of Public Hearings on the Upper Colorado River Storage Project. Vols. 1–8, 1949–1956. Salt Lake City. Typescript.

Urquhart, Jennifer C. "Floating Through Dinosaur." *National Geographic Traveler* 1 (Spring 1984):104–11.

The Vernal Express.

Victor, Frances Fuller. *The River of the West.* Hartford, Conn.: Columbian Book Co., 1870.

WAMOC Rambler, Official Publication of the Wasatch Mountain Club. Salt Lake City: July 1957. Newsletter.

Warner, Ted J., ed. *The Dominguez–Escalante Journal: Their Expedition Through Colorado, Utah, Arizona and New Mexico in 1776.* Translated by Fray Angelico Chavez. Edited by Ted J. Warner. Provo: Brigham Young University Press, 1976.

Weeks, Carl. Papers. University of Utah Marriott Library, Salt Lake City.

"What Is Your Stake in Dinosaur?" Sierra Club, n.d. Brochure.

"Wildlife Experts on Echo Park Dam." Grand Junction, Colorado: Upper Colorado River Grass Roots, Inc., n.d. Brochure.

Woolley, Ted. Telephone conversation with Roy Webb, 9 May 1985.

Zwinger, Ann. *Run, River, Run: A Naturalist's Journey Down One of the Great Rivers of the West.* New York: Harper and Row, 1975.

Index